WAAF

WITH WINGS

Y. M. Lucas

GMS ENTERPRISES

First Published in 1992
by GMS Enterprises
67 Pyhill
Bretton
Peterborough
England
Tel (0733) 265123

ISBN 1 870384 16   4

Body of text set in Helvetica 12 pt
on Apple Macintosh DTP system

Printed for GMS Enterprises by
Woolnough Limited
Express Works,
Church Street
Irthlingborough
Northants
England

CONTENTS

FOREWORD

by

Air Vice-Marshal Geoffrey Eveleigh CB OBE RAF (retd)

I confess to a personal interest because my brother was married to 'one of them', but I can heartily commend thi s excellent narrative of the wartime adventures of an elite little band of flyers; for adventures they were!

It is one thing to drone along in a familiar aircraft in fine weather, enjoying the scenery as it slides away under you - but it is quite another to be contour-chasing in a strange aircraft with a lowering cloudbase and no radio!

Today's pilots with modern aids would regard themselves as foolhardy to get into situations which these girls had to accept as part of their job and which cost Amy Johnson (and others) their lives.

My hat is off to them as they didn't have to do it, but they did it well, and their story belongs in the annals of aviation history.

Geoff. Eveleigh.

21st June 1992

ABBREVIATIONS USED

Adj	Adjutant
Admin	Administration
ATA	Air Transport Auxiliary.
CFI	Chief Flying Instructor
CO	Commanding Officer
FAA	Fleet Air Arm
IAS	Island Air Services
MAP	Ministry of Aircraft Production
MET	Meteorological
MT	Motor Transport
MU	Maintenance Unit
RAF	Royal Air Force
RAFVR	Royal Air Force Volunteer Reserve
RFS	Reserve Flying School
WAAF	Womans Auxiliary Air Force

INTRODUCTION

This is an account of seventeen girls who were in the Women's Auxiliary Air Force during the war, and who were selected and released to the Air Transport Auxiliary (ATA) for training as pilots. They were all taught to fly from scratch and, owning to their very specialised training, were all ferrying any type of light aircraft within six months, and fifteen of them were ferrying Spitfire and other fighter aircraft within a year of their first solo flight. Their names were:-

First intake - 21 February 1944
Rosemary Bonnet
Suzanne Chapman
Yvonne Margaret Eveleigh (Peggy)
Diana Faunthorpe
Joyce Fenwick
June Farquhar
Barbara Lankshear
Patricia Provis (Pat)
Ruth M H Russell
Frances Rudge (Frankie)
Winifred Stokes (Pooh)

plus two who had to retire from the initial training period on medical grounds

A second intake occurred on 8 May 1944. These were:
Sue Alexander
Henrietta Arthur (Henry)
Aimee de Neve
Betty Keith-Jopp
Annette Mahon
Kathleen Stanley-Smith (Katie)

Most still have their log-books and other certified documents, so the dates and details of aircraft flown etc are correct.

CHAPTER ONE
WAAF Days

The Director of the London College of Secretaries looked at the slim, shy girl in front of him and said 'Do you really have to earn your living as a typist? I may as well be quite frank with you, you are the worst pupil we have ever had here. Whatever else you may do in life, I don't think you'll ever be a typist'.

Failure when you are young and keen is devastating. The girl, in spite of biting hard on the inside of her cheeks, could not prevent the tears coming to her eyes as she left his office hurriedly. A few years later she was flying Spitfires.

'Which all goes to show' as her great Aunt Emily said. To show what? That failure should never be allowed to get you down? Or that war can give people opportunities that they would never had had otherwise? Probably being born at the right time and place had something to do with it.

In 1939, at the outbreak of war, most women and girls in England wanted to do something to help. Some were still at school and too young or prevented by family or other commitments to join any of the forces, but volunteered for full or part-time, working in nursing, as VADs or Red Cross, ambulance drivers, land army etc. A very few, rich enough, or lucky enough to have learnt to fly and even to have possessed their own aircraft volunteered to join the Air Transport Auxiliary.

This was the newly formed civilian organisation under British Airways to provide a pool of civilian pilots to fly communications aircraft and to help the Royal Air Force in ferrying and delivering. There were a number of experienced males, commercial and other pilots who were too old, or considered medically unfit to be accepted into the RAF. At first, only men were taken on, but finally, thanks largely to Pauline Gower, eight women were

Miss Pauline Gower MBE, Head of the Womens Section of the Air Transport Auxilliary in the rear cockpit of a DH82 Tiger Moth. Note the fur gloves!

enroled on 1 January 1940, to form an all-women's ferry pool at Hatfield in order to deliver Tiger Moths, the main Air Force trainer at the time. They all had considerable flying experience, and all were qualified flying instructors.

Many other women pilots with pre-war licences had to wait until these first eight had proved their reliability before being allowed to join them and some, meanwhile, in despair, opted for other non-flying wartime jobs. Some women with family or other bonds with the RAF, or who thought that they might get a chance to fly themselves eventually, joined up in the Women's Auxiliary Air Force (WAAF) which had been formed at the end of June 1939.

Early on these were all volunteers and recruited to a limited number of trades, such as administrative, balloon operators, fabric workers, telephonists, drivers, cooks, clerks, mess orderlies and equipment assistants. A few with suitable degrees were given direct commissions as officers in the Meteorological Forecasting Section.

Sue Alexander

Life in the WAAF in the early days was often chaotic, sometimes boring and sometimes hilarious. Sue Alexander was the first to join of the future pilots. She had wanted to learn to fly and wanted to join the Civil Air Guard before the war, but without success. When the war started:

"It seemed the obvious thing to join the WAAF, so I did, at Cranwell. They had enough drivers, so the only thing offered was equipment. We were issued with berets, macs, grey stockings and black shoes. Outdoors we looked more-or-less uniform, but very odd when we took off the macs with the shoes and stockings under civilian skirts! The Equipment Section was run by civilian men who were not a bit pleased to see us. They grudgingly trained us to take over, giving us the most menial and boring jobs, so boredom was quite a problem. One was expecting some excitement.

That winter was called 'the phoney war'. The accommodation was some huts and airmens' married quarters houses. It was a cold winter and Cranwell was very exposed, so that in the houses all the pipes froze. We were allowed home at weekends and on one occasion I came back to find the whole of the ground floor an ice-rink. In spite of these conditions, the only illness was an epidemic of German Measles! On the plus side, we ate in the Airmens Mess and the food was very good. I have never eaten better steak before or since".

Afterwards she was sent to a balloon centre in Essex and later still became a Clerk S/D in plotting, radar and Ops.

A fire-drill was remembered at Bridgenorth when, during a demonstration to the whole camp of a large airfield-type foam extinguisher, it would not turn on. Eventually with the help of hammers and chisels, something gave, and foam gushed out. Unfortunately, nothing would stop it!. The WAAF watched, shaking with uncontrollable laughter while the entire parade ground and the path leading to it was covered with foam. There was no more drill that day!

On another occasion the Camp C.O. put out an order saying 'WAAF must pay more attention to their blackouts as chinks in same could lead to enemy action'. He was unaware that the WAAF also called their issue bloomer-type knickers with elastic around the bottoms, 'blackouts'!

Ruth Russell
Ruth Russell (Hons degree in Geography) says:

"My entry was because my professor at King's College, London, was asked to recommend 'any female fit for the job'. I did not apply, I was asked for. We had two weeks at Loughborough College in an attempt to teach us how to wear uniforms and salute - also to learn how to march, but as I have, ever since a child, fallen flat on my face if I have to stand still, I was released from that on my first day".

In October 1941 she was sent to Gloucester for a three months intensive training in Met. Forecasting. Later she was posted as a forecaster to Cranage, at that time the senior Navigation School.

"I had to do quite a lot of lecturing on Met. to all navigators in training, including the specialist navigation course for senior officers... most of these were Wing Commanders or Group Captains with medals galore".

After, she was posted to Kidlington as Officer-in-Charge of the Met office:
"Where, according to my new C.O. I arrived illegally by air, complete with bicycle, dog and luggage, having been sent that way by my old C.O. I had done some flying as a passenger in my duties, considered necessary to get a complete understanding with pilots I was sending up. Night fog was a big problem, the difference between vertical and approach vision".

From Kidlington, when eventually an Air Ministry order invited applications from the WAAF for ab initio training as pilots she applied, along with some 2,000 others.

Rosemary Bonnet

Rosemary Bonnet joined the WAAF in 1941 after her husband, Dorian Bonnet, failed to return to Scampton, where he was a pilot after a sortie to Essen. She was in the Met. Section as an airwoman. Her friend Maggie Nicholas, gives a graphic description of her:
"I was a corporal in the Met. Office at Scampton and the

WAAF Officer told me there was a new WAAF joining my section and that she was the widow of Flt Lt Bonnet and would I help her as much as possible. I thought it was a pretty daft idea to send anyone to the station where their husband had been so recently killed, but needless to say I didn't give my opinion. I expected quite a sad little person arriving and had the shock of my life when I met Rosie. We were a peaceful section - I was 19, and from that day onwards life was quite traumatic! Rosie was, to us, very glamorous. She knew nearly all the Senior Officers on the station through her husband - and she had never heard of standing orders. I had to get her out of all sorts of scrapes ("You did say you would look after me Maggie") When the AOC came round the Mess and asked her if the meat was alright, she replied 'Yes Sir, but I did think I heard it neigh, didn't you Corporal?'. The Station Warrant Officer looked as if he was going to explode and Group Captain Whitworth had an attack of coughing. Another time, on a Monday night (domestic night) she came in when we had all got our floor spaces in perfect shape, walked all over them and announced that she had bought a horse!.

On the anniversary of Dorian's death, she asked me to go to the Cathedral with her for a service, so off we set, all polished and shining. She gave me a nudge in the middle of the service and whispered 'Didn't you hear?' 'Hear what' I asked. 'Dorian sitting up there laughing at me'. Unfortunately Rosie and the Senior Met. Officer did not get on, so she was posted to Bardsley and later put in an application for pilot training".

Frankie Rudge
Frankie Rudge was a Canadian, but living with her family in the USA after her father was transferred there. She used her British Passport to get a passage to the U.K. "On a banana boat which had called into Montreal for repairs from Kingston, Jamaica. We joined a convoy of 105 ships at Halifax, Nova Scotia. I met Fergus

Horsburgh (my future husband) on this boat as he was coming over to join the RAF. Oh, fate! I dont recall any fear of submarines, but I do remember being told that some ships had been sunk. We were young - I remember we played Bridge and drank Rum! We landed at Belfast and I immediately went to the Air Ministry and said 'Here I am!'".

Frances 'Frankie' Rudge wearing her WAAF Officers uniform.

She started out as an ACW2 recruit Admin and then became in charge of recruits herself as she was offered a NCO's course or the Officers training course at Loughborough.

'I wrote to my father and asked him what I should do and his answer was that he would rather I be a good sergeant than a poor officer. So I decided to be a good officer!

It was December 1941 when I finished the course and was posted to Coastal Command at Greenock. Met a lot of nice Australians there too! My second posting was to RAF Loughborough, where the WAAF Officers had their initial training courses. This time I was WAAF in charge of the small contingent of Airwomen that looked after the Instructors. There was also a RAF Officer Commanding - Wing Commander Paull. I think because there were RAF courses there also. I persuaded him that it would be morale-boosting for the WAAF personnel to meet him and he agreed to have a WAAF inspection parade one morning at 1100 hrs. That particular morning I stopped in to see the WAAF Adjutant until it was time to meet the Wing Commander at the place designated. After talking a while, the WAAF Officer asked me at what time I was meeting the Wingco. When I said 11.00am. she looked at her watch "it is now precisely 11.00am'. My watch had stopped at 10.45!

By the time I arrived my WAAF sergeant was taking the Wing Commander around the three ranks of airwomen, I saluted and apologised. He gave me a dirty look and practically ignored me for the rest of the inspection. As he left, he said "Come and see me in my office". So I did and explained why I had been late for parade. All was forgiven and he took me for a drink at the Bulls Head that evening".

She was a Church Fenton in Yorkshire when she applied for flying training in the ATA.

Peggy Eveleigh

Peggy Eveleigh was another widow whose husband had been killed flying in 1940, only nine months after their wedding. She had always been keen on flying and her husband had given her an 'A' Licence for a wedding present. She had been due to start flying lessons in August 1939, just as civilian flying was stopped on account of the imminent conflict. After taking over the Mastership of the North Somerset Foxhounds for a season, she joined the WAAF. As a recruit she did two weeks training at Innsworth and was then posted to another recruiting depot, Bridgenorth, as acting Corporal in charge of a hut. Here she had to put 30 civilian girls through the same equipping and training as she had done the previous fortnight herself.

"My first attempts at drill were horrific and the

Station Warrant Officer in charge lost his temper with me. However, after being sent on an NCO's course this improved a bit and I was promoted to Corporal. Bridgenorth was an interesting experience to say the least. We were getting the maximum intake and the first conscripts from every walk of life. Of course, mistakes were made - I was sent to meet three cooks at Wolverhampton railway station late one night in a small transport car. The train was late. When it pulled in a whole lot of WAAF disembarked, including a WAAF Sergeant who said 'Here are your 30 cooks'. I said 'I'm only getting three!' 'It says 30 on this form, all for Bridgenorth, here is the list of names'. So saying she got back on the train, leaving me standing with 30 WAAF.

I tried to phone the Duty Officer, but could get no reply. An Army Transport Officer eventually came to my rescue and conjured up a large van. Arriving back at Bridgenorth well after midnight, I made myself most unpopular waking up sergeants and corporals to find beds. We got a disgruntled store-keeper up to provide blankets but as there were not nearly enough beds, it was the floor for most of them that night.

Another time, after the latest intake had been given all their equipment and gone out, I found one poor conscript in tears on her bed, surrounded by her rather daunting issue underwear. I asked her why she was so miserable. 'Oh no Madam, I'm so happy. I've never had new clothes ever before'. I told her to call me Corporal and found out that she was an orphan, brought up by a non-caring relative in Cinderella conditions in Liverpool; cast-off clothing and cleaning floors had been her lot.".

Soon after, Peggy was recommended for a commission. When asked whether she would prefer Intelligence or Administration and, thinking that whatever she said she would probably get the opposite, she said:

"I joined the WAAF in the hope that we might be able to fly one day. Until that happens, I will do whatever you decide will be most useful".

She was given a commission in Intelligence and posted to Air Ministry.

WAAF Clerks were replacing many men, releasing them for flying or other duties, but Clerks S/D (Special Duties) were something different. These were girls employed on sometimes very secret work and were chosen for intelligence, reliability and discretion. Some were employed as 'plotters' with mini croupier's rakes on the underground tables of Command HQ, so that the controllers could decide what action to take. They needed calmness and speed - and to be 'unflappable' as the expression went - under extreme pressure. Others were Radar Operators, Code and Cypher Clerks, Operations Assistants etc. All involved qualities likely to help make a good pilot, which accounts for the fact that the majority of the WAAF who were ultimately chosen for flying training came from these branches.

Diana Faunthorpe

Diana Faunthorpe was a plotter at Fighter Command HQ during the Battle of Britain, then a tracer, trying to record all the plots which happened on the table. After, she was posted to Debden and during her first evening on duty there the airfield was bombed.

"We emerged from the Ops Room to find bomb craters everywhere and to learn that the WAAF quarters had been partially destroyed. We spent the night at the C.O's house, sleeping on the floor, chairs etc. The next day we moved off camp to a requisitioned schoolhouse nearby, sleeping tightly packed in dormitories."

Later, she was commissioned and sent as Movements Liaison Officer to Inverness:

"The job - to identify all tracks as they appeared on the table as to whether friendly or hostile. If declared hostile, local fighter planes were sent up to investigate or shoot down. We didn't have much hostile movement but there was the odd one that sneaked in".

Katie Stanley Smith

Katie Stanley Smith joined the WAAF in December 1941 and, after training at the Met. School in London, was posted to Aldergrove in Northern Ireland.

"I was the first woman in the still civilian Met Office. I was NOT wanted. However, they had little choice in the matter and, as I knew my stuff, they gradually accepted me. Eventually, all the Observers were replaced by women and I became the Corporal-in-Charge. When, in due course, I was posted to the new airfield at Nutts Corner to set up the Met.Office there from scratch, the Head Forecaster made a big commotion and said he could not do without me. Again, he had no choice.

Whilst at Aldergrove I wangled my first ever flight - from Langford Lodge to Hendon - in the rear turret of a Wellington! I spent my spare time with the station Concert Party. Nutts Corner was half British, half American; that is where I met my future husband, he was in the US Weather Office and also spent his free time with the Concert Party.

I bought an old bike and when I had a 48 hour pass I'd put the bike on the train and go exploring; this way I got to know Donegal, Connemara and Dublin. It was marvellous to go to the Free State - lights were on, there were no ration books and one could buy silk stockings, chocolate and lot of other things not available in the United Kingdom. We were not allowed to bring such things across the border, so we got very inventive about smuggling - wearing several pairs of stockings and hanging boxes of chocolates outside the train window during Customs checks. I fell in love with Ireland.

There was talk of sending MET.WAAF to Gibraltar and Cairo. I was endeavouring to be one of those sent when the possibility of flying training in ATA came up. I wanted to join mainly for adventure! My brother was a fighter pilot. As a child I spent many afternoons with him at Croydon aerodrome, watching planes land and take-off, so I was very aware of flight"

It may be possible for you to fly...

By 1941 quite a few women pilots had been recruited for the ATA, the first ones having proved that they were just as reliable and efficient as the men. Winifred Crossley had been the first woman to fly an RAF Fighter - a Hurricane. Five more women were checked out on that aircraft and the women at last were able to do the same work as the men.

Joan Hughes became a flying instructor for both sexes on all aircraft, eventually including four-engined bombers. As there was already a shortage of pilots, the number of trained civilians with flying licences suitable for the ATA was becoming exhausted.

It was decided to take some specially selected men and women and train them from scratch. In the summer of 1942, an Initial Flying Training Unit was set up at Barton-in-the-Clay, a small grass airfield on the edge of the Chiltern hills, where Joan Hughes moved with her pupils and aircraft until called away to instruct on Class II aircraft at White Watham. Captain H W Woods was in charge; he had flown in World War One, and later as an

Imperial Airways pilot.

The ATA gave some of their ground staff the opportunity, and those with the right qualifications were accepted and trained. Also others who had previously applied and shown keeness. The RAF also agreed to release some selected WAAF to train ab initio, the requirements being that they should be under 30 years of age, at least 5"5" in height, pass the RAF Aircrew medical and have at least School Certificate or Matriculation. An Air Ministry Order to that effect was published on 29 July 1943.

By 4 September nearly 1400 applications had been received, which later increased to nearly 2000. To make a 'short list' all those between 23 and 26 years old with matriculation or degrees were picked out. This gave 87 possibles. It was then suggested that this number should be increased to 150 and this was obtained by reducing the lower age limit to 22. These were boarded by MAP - the Ministry of Aircraft production - who were to select 60. By 14 January 1944 31 had been boarded, selected and sent to ATA for interviews.

Barbara Lankshear

The RAF Aircrew medical examinations caused some anxiety. Barbara Lankshear remembers going for hers:

"It was in some warren of a building in London. Going from room to room along very bleak corridors, the only woman with a batch of airmen - weighing, measuring, jumping on and off chairs, ears nose and throat inspections and wondering just how far this batch processing was going to go and whether maybe I was in the wrong building! Luckily, it was not beyond the less intimate things. I was mightily relieved to see another WAAF - also apparently solo - in a group of airmen in the distance at the end of one of those corridors. I found out later that it was Ruth Russell. She and I had a small perk later, in that being Met.Officers we did not have to attend the ATA Met. lectures".

Peggy, who was a bare 5'4" says:
"We had to be 5'5", so I cut out two soles of the thickest chiropodists' felt I could buy and put them on my feet under my thick grey airforce stockings. I knew from previous experience that they usually weighed and measured you first, making you take off your shoes, but not undress; this came later behind a screen, when the 'soles' could be peeled off with the stockings, leaving your feet bare to be 'tickled' by the examining Medical Officer who was presumably testing your reactions!"

A bunch of those who passed their medical were sent for further interviews at MAP. We waited in a library while we were called in one by one. Ruth Russell came out and we asked her what they had wanted to know. She said they had asked her questions on engines which she could'nt answer. She had said: 'How do you expect me to remember with all you men sitting there terrifying me?'

Pat Provis

She went through the same selection procedure. Whilst in the library, she carefully noted the titles of one or two books on aircraft technology. When asked, she said she had read those books and learned quite a lot from them. She put her selection down to 'being a good liar!' She was not the

only one...

Peggy, when asked if she knew anything about engines replied that she had done a course at the Chelsea Technical College. What she omitted to say was that this was only for a couple of hours and had been arranged by the British School of Motoring when she was taking a driving course there! The interview board said that 'she probably knew more than they did' - and asked no further questions on engines or mechanics!

Katie:

"I think I was chosen because I had the correct English education, passing School Certificate with a good matriculation, and I think I displayed self-confidence in my interview. I had been at home in Croydon during the Battle of Britain, and saw the first bombs that fell on Croydon in the air!.

I joined the Women's Land Army in March 1941 and took care of the pigs and chickens at a Mental Institute at Teddington. I had two mental inmates as my helpers - one was prone to epileptic fits and the other was a religious maniac who preached sermons to the pigs. At my first Air Ministry interview someone there made a crack looking at my record, that it was a long way from Land Army to Ferry Pilot!'

The administration and selection having taken several months, meanwhile the ATA had been told that they would be loaned RAF personnel who were already trained pilots no longer suitable for operations or not quite up to standard. These would be temporarily released from the RAF. The arrangements previously made for the intake of some 30 women from the WAAF would not be affected however.

The ATA could now afford to be very exacting, and they were. Of 31 sent down to White Waltham for interview, only 13 were accepted. The shrinkage from the original 31 was partly due to a few last-minute withdrawals, but also the results of medical examinations, psychological tests and interviews at White Waltham. It was agreed that further selections should be made to bring the numbers up to the 30 agreed upon. On 15 April, further WAAF attended White Waltham for interviews and examinations, of whom only 6 were chosen. No further interviews followed.

Barbara:
"... the Psychological Intelligence Test there was a big blackboard on which was a diagram of the plumbing of a building: taps, stop-cocks, tanks, baths. You had to fill a bath or get water out of a certain tap without it spurting out anywhere else by turning on and off the appropriate inlets and outlets"

Peggy:
"The Medical Officer explained it to me briefly and told me to fill the bath with hot water and the lavatory cistern with cold. He then busied himself writing. I looked at the problem: it was quite simple, there were a couple of 'catches' where one had to be careful. I remembered the simple square peg in the round hole type of test I had had to do five times in the WAAF, the fifth time not taking it very seriously for I had deliberately put bicycle wheels on railway engines and vice versa, which looked more fun!

I thought they were never looked at, but was hauled up before the 'Trick Cyclist' (the name given to the RAF Psychologists) and reprimanded for my perverted sense of humour. As I remembered this a smile came to my face which was noticed by the ATA Officer who said 'I suppose you think this is rather childish, but it is not unlike the hydraulic or petrol system in an aircraft'.

I dared not tell him the real reason for my grin, but I could see his point and applied myself seriously to the test"

June Farquhar:

"Kitty Farrer, Pauline Gower's Second -in- Command was Master of the Aldenham Harriers and lived fairly close. I saw quite a lot of her for a while, a super woman. My first interview in ATA was with her, as Pauline was ill that day. She remembered my little black mare that I hunted, and told me to wear extra high heels for any further interviews! But at least my  medicals went through ATA with my height as 5'5" - it was actually 5 feet 2 inches!".

The first 13 WAAF selected by ATA for training received instructions that they would be temporarily released from the WAAF on 21 February 1944 and were to report to White Waltham at 10.00hrs on that date.

" Most of us met up for the first time here, and could hardly believe our luck! We were put on a bus and driven to Haddenham, near Thame where ATA had their training school. We were quartered on a site quite close to the airfield, a solid hut with separate canteen building. Compared to some of the WAAF accommodation we had experienced, it was almost luxurious. We each had our own bedroom, rather spartanly equipped with iron bedstead and 'biscuit type' mattresses, but there were bathrooms at the end of the hut and a sitting room, thoughtfully equipped with an ironing board.

We were given an introductory talk by an officer who explained to us that we would do two weeks ground school before starting flying. He told us in no uncertain terms that we would survive entirely on our own merits. We had elected to do a man's job and would be treated as men. Parachutes were heavy and aircraft often parked a long way away. We could not expect to be helpless females and get things carried for us. If we made stupid mistakes we would suffer the consequences, there would be neither prejudice or favouritism because we were women. If any of us behaved in an undisciplined manner, or did anything contrary to ATA rules and regulations, we were likely to be sent back to the WAAF. 'If that happens...' he said, ...I couldn't care less'

Later, whilst walking back to our billet, we discussed the possibility of going into one of the local pubs for a drink. We decided that perhaps it would be better not to do this, at any rate so early on in the course, as it might create a bad impression. 'Remember...' someone said, '...I couldn't care less'

This expression was in common use in the ATA, and very often meant the exact opposite!"

CHAPTER TWO
Initial Training

Ground Instruction for the trainees was in a hut on the edge of the airfield. They were taught the essentials of aircraft and their engines, the theory of flight, meteorology, navigation, ferrying procedure, parachutes and their use and many other things. It was sometimes difficult to concentrate when outside there was a continuous stream of aircraft taking off and landing. Training was carried out on Percival Proctors and noisy North American Harvards. Miles Magisters were taking off and landing on cross-countries; No.1 Ferry Pool was carrying out their usual flights with Fairchild and Avro Anson taxi planes to deliver and collect their pilots, and there was the odd Spitfire occasionally taking off or landing. The girls watched enviously and wondered if any of them would get that far.

All were all longing to get over to Barton, a small grass airfield where the initial training took place. They were issued with flying clothing - wonderful brown suede flying boots, leather gauntlets with white silk gloves to go inside, goggles, flying helmets... The Maps and Signals Office gave an explanation as to their importance to ferry pilots, keeping daily up to date information on the state of airfields, whereabouts of barrage balloons, firing ranges, prohibited flying areas, obstructions and a mass of other useful and often essential information. They also provided two sets of flying maps for the British Isles - one on a small scale and the other much larger. The trainees were told to keep these carefully and report any loss immediately as they were highly secret.

Finally the great day came when, on a fine March morning, they piled into the bus with all their equipment for the first of their daily journeys to Barton-in-the-Clay. It was a tiny grass airfield nestling under the Chiltern hills off the main Bedford road. There was a single building

27

with a large general room, a locker room,cloakrooms, kitchen and a couple of small offices for the CO and Instructors. Each girl was allocated a locker and introduced to their flying Instructors. Each Instructor had about three or four pupils. The aircraft were Miles Magisters; small, low wing monoplanes which were parked around the airfield, or under Blister hangars. The Instructors told them in which order they were to fly and then took each girl up individually for their first lesson - this was on the effect of controls and straight and level flying. The first day was fine, they were all thrilled to actually be in the air and most made steady progress during the first week. All, that is, except one girl, who was airsick every time she went up! Unavailingly, she stuffed her flying overalls with paper bags, but it was no use. She had to give up eventually and departed sorrowfully, reducing the number to twelve, which pleased the more superstitious!

March weather stopped some of the flying days. When conditions were impossible owing to low cloud, they would be sent back early, and spent the afternoons going for walks in the rain, discussing their flying progress (or lack of it) or doing domestic jobs in their sitting room. In April, the majority had their first solo flight. Joyce Fenwick, dark, calm and elegant was the first; Winifred Stokes - who was always known as 'Pooh' was the second.

Ruth Russell was ready for solo when her Instructor went on leave... "Instead S/O Codlin was to take me up for a few minutes and went to what he thought was a safe low-flying area. He was not in the right place!. We hit high-tension cables and the plane fell to the ground'.

Peggy Eveleigh takes up the story:
"I was sent for by the CO. He said to me 'I believe you are the senior WAAF Officer here. As you have probably heard, Ruth and her Instructor had a crash this morning; they are both in hospital. She is not seriously injured, but I

think it would be a good idea if you went down and visited her'. I agreed and drove down to the hospital with the CO. Ruth was in a ward by herself. Like most patients, she wanted to tell me all about it. I had been a VAD nurse and done a course in hospital at the beginning of the war and knew this helped. She said her Instructor had taken over control and had said that he would show her some low flying".

As Ruth explained:
"I was just sitting there as a passenger, not touching the controls. Low flying always frightened me a bit and suddenly he flew slap into some wires. The next thing I knew, we were on the ground. I realised I was not badly hurt and climbed out, then came the awful part. My Instructor was in the front cockpit and his leg was trapped and horribly twisted. I could do nothing to get him out, or to help him - and nobody came. I shouted for help but there seemed to be nothing but deserted fields all around. I knew there was a First Aid kit in the plane, but I could not find it. I suppose I must have been quite dazed myself, my head was feeling very queer and I was bleeding quite a lot. My Instructor was screaming in pain and shouting for Morphia. When I did eventually find the First Aid kit, I could not find any Morphia in it. Finally, a farmer came and then went off again for help. It seemed ages before the Ambulance came and I have never known a more horrible time in my life".

Peggy:
"Poor Ruth, a terrible start to her flying career and one for which she was in no way responsible. I said that no doubt her parents and relatives would be coming to see her and I would return as soon as possible. She said 'All I want to do is go home. I can walk, nothing is broken and they have fixed my ear'.

Ruth left hospital two days later, but collapsed on the way home and was taken to Leatherhead Cottage

Hospital with delayed concussion. This was 20 April, and it says much for her determination and courage that she was back flying again on 2 June. She went solo, then was back at Haddenham on Proctors in August, was ferrying Class I aircraft in November and flew her first Spitfire on 19 April 1945, within a year of her accident. She continued ferrying Class I and II aircraft until the ATA disbanded at the end of September 1945.

Before going solo they had to have a check with the Chief Instructor, Captain Wood, or 'Woody' as he was affectionately known to most of us. This was usually a worse ordeal that the first solo flight. Apart from the fact that one was automatically nervous, he had the habit of making comments, which for those with helmets too large for them were difficult to hear and could be off-putting - particularly on the final approach! One of the last to go solo, after having failed her first check, was told by her Instructor to pretend she was taking up a passenger. This worked, and Captain Woods would have been very surprised if he knew that every time he said something, his pupil would say to herself 'It is his first flight; he does not know what he is talking about!' After doing three satisfactory circuits and landings, he stepped out of the aircraft and sent her off alone!

Next followed a period of instruction on steep turns, forced landings, turning onto compass courses, dual navigation, cross country and a host of other things, interspersed with periods of solo practice. It was now May 1944 and D-Day was coming up. Of course, it was a closely guarded secret, so our airfield was not informed until it was well under way - with the result that a couple of the Instructors when they heard immediately got airborne with a cross-country exercise to the South Coast!. June Farquhar, a former Radio Operator and Peggy were the two lucky pupils, with their Instructors Coltman and Adams respectively. They had taken off before the order was given that all aircraft had to be grounded that day.

June:
"The D-Day episode with Coltman was absolutely rivetting. We flew down the coast from Margate to Portsmouth. For one thing, he flew the aircraft after we got to the coast and so I was free to take in the whole scene. Flying along the coastline, about 100 feet from the shore, there was the most incredible beauty, seeing the shells explode with great orange fireballs when they hit a boat. There was no noise above the Magister's engine and it did not seem real or lethal at that stage. That came later... Seeing sections of the great Mulberry Harbour being towed from their places of construction, wondering and trying to figure out how it was going to be used - why we were allowed to tootle along, heaven only knows, I guess that everyone was too busy to notice us".

Peggy:
"We went from Dover to Shoreham and I was amazed to see ships in the Channel shooting or being shot at; little plumes of water jetting up from the sea where the shells had fallen short. Visibility was good and they looked like little toys. Three German aircraft coming out of the cloud cover above us sent us diving towards the ground, but they either did not notice us or were perhaps occupied with more important things!"

In May The girls were joined by the final six WAAF to be accepted for ab initio training by the ATA. Sue Alexander was one of these... "I knew I was lucky to get 'Smithy' as an Instructor, he really enjoyed it. The only thing I did not care for was that he loved flying upside down, and my parachute always seemed to slip forward so that he could not get his stick back to get the right way up again - he thought it was a great joke!"

And Katie... "I well remember my first evening at Thame. The first batch had nearly all gone solo I think. Anyway, the 'old girls' were telling us newcomers about the various

Instructors. Someone told me of one, Captain Marks, who liked to fly upside down and I thought to myself 'Heaven preserve me from him!' Of course that was who I got and I would not have exchanged him for the others. He was great and loved flying upside down. I had him again for Class II - I loved doing aerobatics with him when he checked out planes".

Suzanne Chapman

Suzanne Chapman, petite, dark, vital and very keen had started off in the WAAF ranks like most of the girls. She had been commissioned in 1942 and had been at No.8 Maintenance Unit at Little Rissington in 1943 where she met and talked to many ATA pilots when they collected or delivered aircraft there. She put in her application to join the ATA as soon as the possibility of accepting WAAF was announced.

She and Peggy were in despair when they had not gone solo by the end of April, when most of the others had.

Suzanne with Coltman (her Flying Instructor) at Barton-in-the-Clay during April 1944

However, they both achieved this early in May, after which they had no more trouble. On Proctors they were both instructed by Ian Coutts, a very calm and patient Instructor who later trained several of us on Harvards when we were doing Class II.

Another Instructor, 'Nobby' Pearmund and Ian

were testing a Harvard at Thame one day after it had undergone a major overhaul. During the air test the engine stopped dead. Fortunately this happened near the airfield, whereupon Nobby was able to show his skills by doing a perfect forced landing, wheels and flaps down.

Ian Coutts said the most dangerous thing that happened to him at Haddenham was not whilst flying, but in playing mixed hockey against the WAAF. "I had my eyebrow spilt open and injuries were sustained by other male participants - a most dangerous game, mixed hockey!"

The ATA training scheme was the brilliant work of ARO Mac Millan, who had formerly been the Chief Flying Instructor of British Airways. He had prepared an efficient and comprehensive schedule, helped by Bill Gribble and others which enabled pilots to fly any type of aircraft safely in just about a year.

A ferry pilot, to be useful, had to be able to ferry any type without doing a conversion course on each new type. No aerobatics, instrument flying, formation flying or night flying were included, as this was not necessary for pilots whose sole job was to deliver aircraft safely and undamaged. Calmness and efficiency were demanded, not the ability to be daring and take risks. Mac Millan was not biased against women pilots and was prepared to accept anyone who could fly competently and reliably. By the time the WAAF entry came in, women had already more than proved their capabilities. Lettice Curtis, Joan Hughes, Rosemary Rees and several others had already qualified on four-engined bombers; Lettice, who gives a full description in her book 'The Forgotten Pilots', alone delivered over 300 of them. Joan Hughes instructed both sexes on them. Altogether eleven women ferried these four-engined monsters without accident.

The flying school at Thame turned out pilots who had flown four different types of light aircraft - in the WAAF case, Magisters, Tiger Moths, Proctors and

Fairchilds - and had completed courses in navigation, meteorology, airframes, engines, and ferrying procedures. They were then given their wings and sent out solo on some 20 cross-country flights, the last ones being to Scotland or similar, to give them practice in finding their way about England in the air without the help of any sort of radio communication with the ground.

All had to fly within ATA limits - 2000 yard visibility and 800 feet above the ground. All were taught low-level circuits and precautionary landings in the event of an emergency. The ATA approach was a long one with the engine 'on' although they were taught glide approaches and landings, but only for the purpose of forced landings through engine failure.

After the cross country flights the pilots were posted to No. 5 Ferry Pool, also at Thame, where they were progressively given other types of Class I aircraft, as well as taxi jobs on the Fairchild Argus, delivering other pilots.

At the end of training at Barton they had a check-flight with 'Woody' the CO. who usually made the pilot take him to a designated point on the local map, with steep turns flown on the way and cutting the throttle suddenly to simulate engine failure. The pilot then had to put the aircraft into a glide and choose and point out a suitable field to him and make an approach. When he could see that they were going to make it, he would open the throttle again and tell the pilot to carry on.

June:
"Woody lived in Tring and was thus conversant with all our local country and knew where we lived, so on test he flew over the farm and 'cut' the engine. We swooped low over the house, much to the fear of my Mama who was outside watching!. He then did a 'beat up' of the place with steep turns and dives which impressed them all no end - they thought it was me!"

Peggy:

"One by one we all passed out and were ready to start our training at Haddenham. We were all very happy about this. We could all fly a light aircraft and had been paid to learn to do so! We felt incredibly lucky. Ten of us started on Proctors at more or less the same time. One girl, Mary King, had to drop out as she got a nasty bout of Glandular Fever, which put her out for two months or so and she never did return to training"

The Percival Proctor was a quite fast low-wing monoplane, originally designed as a communications machine. It had two fuel tanks and was equipped with a Gipsy Six engine, driving a variable pitch propeller. The aircraft demonstrated a decided tendency to swing into wind when landing crosswind, so care had to be taken. WAAF pilots did their first runway landings on this machine at a nearby RAF station and the design was very good for a training machine, as one learnt to correct an incipient swing before it started.

June:

"I seem to remember clocking up a rather excessive amount of instructional hours with Eric Lambert, due to heading for Marshalls Airport at Cambridge and then taking a punt out on the 'Backs' for a while on lovely summery days. I then suddenly realised it was all going down in my log-book as extra flying time and said 'Enough' - I had no intention of being logged as a slow pupil!"

Frankie:

"When training on Proctors, Ian Coutts was my Instructor. As usual, just when I was enjoying my lesson, the engine died. Ian had cut the motor, indicating that I was to make a trial forced landing.

I spotted a field straight ahead that I thought would do and glided towards it. Lower and lower we came. The Instructor was the one who would judge whether or not that forced landing attempt would be successful and only he would open on full throttle so that we could once again gain height. However, in this case the Proctor was just about to skim over the hedge into the chosen grass field and I thought 'this must be a genuine forced landing' when suddenly Ian opened up the throttle and we climbed up to normal altitude.

When we got back to Thame he looked under the aircraft and sure enough, there was part of the hedge wrapped around the landing wheels!

Since then he has told me he was never so frightened in his life, but the question remains unanswered - whose fault was it?... Anyway, he passed me on to Harvards!"

Forty years later Ian Coutts said that when he opened the throttle the engine did not respond - when he thought a crash was inevitable, the engine suddenly picked up! Ian Coutts instructed a total of 7 WAAF pilots on Proctors at Thame, and later several on Harvards when they came back for the Class II course there. He remembers details of some of the lesser-known aspects of life there...

"The Army asked for our assistance by taking two of their officers up in a Harvard to inspect the camouflage of their transport columns just before D-Day. I took a young Lieutenant up, and being airsick, he had armed himself with several strong paper bags. These he duly dropped on some of his badly camouflaged troops. I would like to point out that I had the highest regard for him, because as soon as he recovered, he asked to be taken up again, armed with more paper bags".

Ian also remembers being caught by the RAF Corporal and his Alsatian guard dog whilst crawling through a gap in the barbed wire fence behind the Mess Hut to get to his car after a party ...

"The ATA doctor - who later married Annette - and myself always took it in turns to drive from Thame village to Haddenham and back, when there was a party in the

Mess. On one occasion it was my turn to drive and at the end of the party I went to collect the car, but it was nowhere to be seen. We searched everywhere without success and I finally 'phoned the Aylesbury police, while the doctor arranged with a rather disgruntled Matron for us to stay in the Sick bay for the night. The next morning a further search proved unproductive, so I went to work. When I landed at 11 o'clock one of the fitters told me that they had found my car - it was wedged firmly behind an air-raid shelter!. It took seven men to lift it out, and I never did find out who was responsible!"

On the whole though, the pilots had less dual time and more time now to practice solo whatever exercises they were told to do. When considered ready, they were given one flight in a De Havilland Tiger Moth and one on a

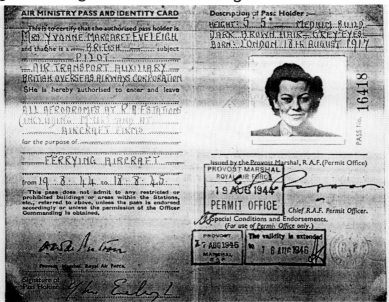

Reproduction of Yvonne Eveleigh's somewhat battered Air Ministry Pass and Identity Card that must have shown hundreds of times. Note that the ATA was part of British Overseas Airways Corporation!

Fairchild Argus without any previous dual on the type, to see how they got on with a strange machine. Finally, they had a test with the CO, who took them on a longer cross-country flight, with precautionary and forced landings on the way. Passing this test, they were issued with an Identity card which allowed them to enter all airfields and factories 'For the purpose of ferrying His Majesty's aircraft'; also a Flight Authorisation card, which allowed them to authorise their own flights. With this card the RAF and Fleet Air Arm could only advise them - they did not have to get their permission to take off.

They were also issued with a small blue book - the ferry pilots 'bible', more of which later. Finally there was an order to Messrs Austin Reed of Regent Street to measure and fit them with two uniforms each - jacket, trousers and skirt - complete with ATA golden wings and cap with gold cap badge. This took a while to be made, so they started the next stage of training, cross country flights, still in civilian clothes.

CHAPTER THREE
Cross-Country Flight

The object of these cross country flights, apart from giving the pilots experience in finding their way around England, was to get used to ferry conditions - landing at strange airfields, being independent and making their own arrangements as regards to re-fuelling, checking on weather and communicating with base. There were some 26 routes laid down; these were on a list that could be studied and we were given about 20 of these. The WAAF pilots were usually allocated different routes so that they could not follow each other. Having been allocated a route and aircraft -invariably a Magister - each pilot was given forms that had to be signed by the Flying Control officers on the airfields they were to land at. Then it was off for a visit to the Maps and Signals and Met.Office to work out the route, drift and course to steer, collect a parachute, overnight bags and a bar of chocolate in case they missed lunch and finally check out with Flying Control.

The Instructors[marked*] and the Staff at Barton (L.to R) Coltman [*], Cowan [*], Lead[*], Adjutant, Sister, Adams [*], Fitzgerald [*] Capt Woods, School C.O. (sitting)

All this took time. If one hurried it was easy to make mistakes as regards to course to steer etc. Peggy decided if you worked out all these flights beforehand, drawing the lines and measuring the courses on the maps, all you had to do on the day was to work out your drift according to the winds as forecast by the Met. Office. She spent three evenings doing this, with the consequence that she was always first away in the mornings and back by lunchtime, asking if she could do a second in the afternoon - which was nearly always possible at first on the short ones. This way she caught up with Joyce Fenwick, who was ahead of her, having been first to solo and was the first to finish cross-country flight.

Frankie:
"On one of my training cross-country flights in the Magister, the weather started to close in and, according to the ATA flying instructions for ferry pilots, I put down at the nearest airfield until it cleared. There was also another ATA pilot who had put in for the same reason as myself. We both sat in the office of the Test Pilot. The ATA pilot was from another ATA pool and was delivering a Spitfire somewhere.

When the weather cleared later in the afternoon, we decided to continue our respective flights and he told me I could take off first, which i did. Having set my compass on the intended course and flying at the prescribed height of 1,000 feet I began to wonder why my map reading was not agreeing with what I saw on the ground below, but I was not really worried at this stage - yet!

However, suddenly I was surprised to see the Spit arrive alongside me, practically standing on its tail to keep pace with the Maggie and me, and the pilot I had met on the ground was waving at me. I waved back. He then gesticulated frantically, pointing backwards. Again, I waved happily to him, think he was just acting crazy for the fun of it. Finally, he flew away - probably, in retrospect, in disgust.

A few minutes later the penny dropped. What he had been trying to tell me was that I had set my compass diametrically opposite to the course I was meant to be on!. So, I shamefacedly turned around, glad that I was all alone and no-one could see me. Yes, I arrived at the proper airfield eventually!

On another cross-country training flight in a Maggie, I landed at some designated airfield, got my chit signed and then taxied to the take-off point on the airfield. When I was given the green light, I put on full power and climbed to about a hundred feet when the engine started to splutter.

We were told that when this happened to land straight ahead. I could not see over the tall trees at the edge of the perimeter straight ahead and probably would have landed just before them, crashing into them, or even landing on top of them. To my right were Blister hangars - no good unless you wanted to be beheaded! Further to my right I spied a space beyond the hangars, small, but empty with a hedge on its father side, before a road and some village houses.

I applied full flap and right rudder and landed just before hitting the hedge. As I nonchalantly(!!!) got out of my Maggie, (my legs could hardly support me) over the hedge came about a dozen American G.I's ! They thought I was going to land on them in the adjacent field and had dived into the hedge for protection!"

Others also had unexpected experiences while doing their cross country flights. June had an engine failure:

"I was lucky, as it was a classic occasion. I had just been doing lots of practice forced-landings that week - it was just before we got our wings, and were still in mufti - so the drill was clear in my mind and a convenient bonfire showed the wind direction and an equally convenient sports ground came into sight amongst the outskirts of Swindon suburbs. But, to see a detachment of Home Guard all surrounding my poor little aircraft now makes me think so much of 'Dads Army'. Brize Norton sent a car to pick me up - the WAAF Adjutant there was a great

June Farquhar stands by Miles Magister '2' at Barton-in-the Clay during April 1944.

school friend of mine and so it was the obvious airfield to get in touch with - and the next day one of Haddenham's instructors flew over and collected me. He was able to reassure me that it was a genuine failure and no fault of mine that the aircraft had to land. Quite a relief! The plane was dismantled and trailered back to base and I got a recommendation for a successful   landing of the Magister.

I can remember the WAAF Officers quizzing me on staying overnight at various stations, some downright jealous and sarcastic, others envious and interested; but then, I suppose there was no reason for them to like us!

How blissful the cross-country trips were - seeing the harvest being gathered and noticing how the contours of the landscape were accentuated by the lines the reapers made in the fields, and the patterns of the corn-stooks. I think I must have wandered many miles off course on so many occasions just to see the wonderful countryside and great estates.

I had a long period of non-flying when I had a really

rotten bout of 'flu and so was grounded from cross-country flying during that while".

Sitting around in the evenings in our small sitting room, we often discussed our luck and why we had been selected amongst so many. We could find nothing that we all had in common, apart from age group, education and physical fitness, which hundreds of others not so lucky had also. Of course, we had no idea as to how the 'short list' had been obtained. We had been questioned on sport; some of us had ridden and hunted, and some had ski-ed - others had done dingy sailing. All were sports that involved a degree of risk and perhaps that developed judgement. We all had wanted to fly.

The ulimate choice by ATA seemed to have depended partly on whether or not we had applied previously. An Air Ministry order dated 4 May 1943 stated "Pilots in the WAAF should, if they wished, be released to ATA and a number have been so released". This had caused a spate of applications to ATA from WAAF with few or no hours - some even inventing them in order to be considered! Some of us were amongst them. Others had had a few lessons, or a fair amount of air experience as passengers, but not all.

We were a very mixed bunch, both Officers and Airwomen. from various parts of the country, with very different characters; some romantic, some authorative, some rather frivolous and others serious and quiet. We all loved the freedom of flying solo, the breathtaking beauty of the sky and the clouds, and the feeling of detachment from all that was going on far down below. We were rewarded by a deep personal satisfaction. It gave many of us a different sense of values. Mankind seemed so small, so insignificant from the realm of infinite space. It was a different world, inhabited by white fluffy clouds, pillars of tall cumulus, dark threatening rain and thunderclouds, and always haze over England - which one could get above on a clear day and be amazed by the clarity above.

In July, some of us had finished Cross Country flight and most of the others, even the six who were on the second entry, had finished their training at Barton. It seemed likely that we would soon separate. We decided to give a party in our small sitting room one Saturday evening to celebrate having learned to fly and, for some, to have got their ATA wings. June decided that it should be called a 'Pink Elephant' party and she drew and cut out large and amusing pink elephants from paper which festooned the walls. Someone with connections in Wales managed to get two large salmon flown in for it - unheard of in wartime! We all produced contributions in the food and drink line from our homes and elsewhere, no mean feat with the strict rationing then in force. We invited all our Instructors, most of whom managed to come. A large fruit punch-bowl was centre point, not too alcoholic; beer was plentiful (it was comparatively weak in wartime too). There was also a small supply of Gin and Whisky. As there was no flying next day we could keep going as long as the food and drink lasted. The Pink Elephants remained on the walls for some time afterwards.

After completing several cross country flights successfully, pupils were then allocated a few long ones, which usually meant an overnight stop. Catterick in Yorkshire was a pre-war permanent RAF Station, and they usually had the most comfortable sleeping quarters. Peggy and Pooh both had interesting experiences when deciding to stop there. When Peggy arrived and circled the airfield, she could see a large cross on the signals square, indicating that no landings could be made there. So she went on to nearby Scorton, only to find it occupied by Americans who had no facilities for putting up women, but they provided a jeep to drive her to Catterick.

On entering the Officers Mess, she was surprised to see Sergeant-Pilots playing Billiards, but thought 'Good, the RAF is getting less formal at last!'. Then she was amazed to see one officer with make-up and lipstick on! 'This...' she thought '...was going a bit too far -

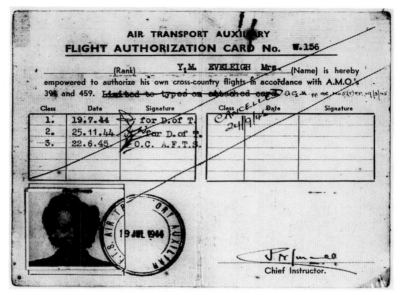

Reproduction of Flight Authorization Card No. W.156 belonging to Mrs Y M Eveleigh that declares that she is '...empowered to authorize his (!) own cross-country flights in accordance with A.M.O.'s

Sergeants fine, but open homosexuality...?' She approached a Flight Lieutenant who looked OK and asked if there was any WAAF accommodation available. She was surprised by his reply 'I've no idea, you better ask one of the RAF'. Seeing her look of complete bewilderment, he said 'I'm just one of the Film Unit'. It appears that they were making the film "Way to the Stars' there, having been lent the station, temporarily without squadrons for the purpose. Most of the occupants of the Mess were actors.

Pooh Stokes, when she spent the night there remembers John Mills coming over to talk to her, and sitting at dinner with him, Michael Redgrave and Richard Attenborough. A way to the stars indeed!

CHAPTER FOUR

First Postings

For those who had finished Cross Country Flight came posting to other Ferry Pools to do 50 hours of taxi-work. This meant flying the Fairchild back from airfields where pilots had gone to collect aircraft and flying it again - empty - to collect them from their delivery destinations. Class I pilots were not allowed to carry passengers and the rule was that the most senior pilot flew the taxi aircraft when there was more than one person in it. In addition, we were given a certain amount of Class I aircraft to ferry, these being all single-engined light aircraft.

Suddenly it seemed that the WAAF pilots might get on to Class II instruction - Harvards and Spitfires - and be able to ferry fighter aircraft. Peggy was posted to White Waltham, which was lucky for her, as it was a busy pool with plenty of taxi work.

"I had a strange billet in a very big, old-fashioned Victorian house on the edge of Maidenhead Thicket. Convenient for the airfield, but the only other occupant was the aged owner who kept saying to me ' I do hope you'll be spared'. I found this slightly disconcerting as I could not think of a suitable reply.

As a result, I spent as much time as possible at the airfield, waiting until dark in case there was a last minute taxi job to do. I felt very junior at White Waltham, which was the headquarters of the ATA as well as being No. 1 Ferry Pool and full of senior Captains and Commanders. Flight Captain Harben, who I flew to collect from his ferrying job, asked me to check him in on arrival at White Waltham. I asked his name: 'Flight Captain HARPIC'. I looked doubtful, thinking he was having me on. "yes, unfortunate but true'. So I went in and wrote Flight Captain HARPIC on the Operations Board - and promptly got ticked off for being cheeky!

The operations officers were extremely nice and

helpful, and when they realised how keen I was to get as much flying in as possible they gave me a lot of extra short taxi work. In this way I soon completed my 50 hours and was sent back to Haddenham in time to get onto the next Class II conversion course in September".

Most were now in uniform and felt very smart in the navy blue jackets and trousers, with gold wings on their breast. They were often not recognised however, and were mistaken for Bus Conductors, Fire Service and many other things. June and Ruth once went into an elegant Department Store in Leicester to go to the 'Ladies' - they were stationed at Ratcliffe at the time - whereupon the attendant took them to the Gas Meters; she thought they were from the Gas Board!"

On the cross country and ferrying flights WAAF pilots had often come up against the problem that many RAF airfields did not have facilities for women, which were sometimes very necessary after a long flight.

June:
"I remember a silly occasion on delivering to one of the Kentish fighter stations. After a long day all I needed was to spend a penny but, great worry, they only had the men's loo. So, Adjutant and CO stood guard while June availed herself. On coming out I found ten of them lining the corridor as a Guard of Honour - and all at attention! One quickly learned not to be shy!"

Ruth:
"One time I was frozen in a Tiger Moth going from the South to the West coast of Scotland. Direction; due North - Wind: a gale from due North - my ground speed was very slow. After three hours I landed somewhere a bit deserted and was immediately dragged from the cockpit frozen. An elderly airman said 'Quick lady, the men's is the closest and I'll stand guard'. I think they were the first words he spoke to me! I was then fed on hot tea with condensed milk and sugar. Medicinal, as I hate it!

47

Most of us came across this problem and when we got our ferry or cross country chits in the morning there would be an immediate dash to the loos as one never knew when the next possibility would present itself. We learnt the wisdom of the Royalties' advice; never lose an opportunity!"

Suzanne Chapman, one of the keenest, was unlucky in being sent to Hamble for her first secondment. This all-women's pool on the south coast had little work for Class I pilots, being mainly engaged in clearing the nearby factories producing fighter-type aircraft. There were very few Class I aircraft to be moved - and not much Fairchild taxi-work - as motor transport was often used to and from Eastleigh and other airfields close by. So there were no new types for Suzanne; Alison King, the Operations Officer, could do little to help her when she continually asked for jobs; she found her month there very frustrating.

Katie, who was posted there in November, found the same: "I was given very little work, and my billet was in a farm in the middle of nowhere. I had transport to and from the airfield, but was stranded once on the farm; could'nt get to a movie, shops or anything".

A lonely month. Her next posting after Christmas was to Sherbourn-in-Elmet in Yorkshire, a mixed pool, where she had Betty for company, which was much better, and they were both sent back to Thame to start their Class II training in March.

"I was seconded to Sherbourn-in-Elmet for Class I ferry work. The whole four weeks I was there the wind was always from the West. so the circuit and runway in use never changed. Later, I delivered an aircraft there, did my usual circuit, landed and wondered vaguely why the Control Van was at the wrong end of the runway!. It was at Sherburn that Betty and I had a billet that fed us baked beans for breakfast, lunch and dinner".

The WAAF pilots gradually split up as they were

posted to other pools for one months' secondment - mainly to White Waltham, Ratcliffe, Cosford, Sherburn and Prestwick. There were 14 Ferry Pools in all, but some of them were against having women, particularly Belfast, Bristol and Lossiemouth, even for a short period.

All on a single card...

The pilots gained a lot of valuable experience flying strange aircraft to all sorts of different aerodromes. All ATA pilots were equipped with a wonderful little blue book called 'Ferry Pilots Notes'. This was a series of postcard sized cards produced by the ATA on each of which was a summary of every type of aircraft in use by the RAF and FAA, in alphabetical order. It gave all the essential facts that the ferry pilot needed to know in order to ferry the aircraft, and the cards were held together by metal rings so that it could be held open at whatever page was needed. Obviously, it was difficult to remember different approach speeds, degrees of flap, stalling speed and all the other details needed on different types. One glance at the appropriate pages gave the pilot everything that was needed, including what type of fuel should be used and the different speeds required for different types of the same aircraft.

When flying a new type for the first time a pilot went to her Flight Captain beforehand who would give her any points that she should pay particular attention to and then go through the handling notes of the type. This was a small booklet that gave a very complete technical description of the aircraft and how to fly it. The essentials of this booklet were condensed into one card contained in the Ferry Pilots Notes. It worked very well and all ATA pilots flew types they had never seen before with no more preparation than this.

Every morning at the Ferry Pools, pilots reported to Operations to get their jobs for the day. RAF 41 Group Central Ferry Control at Andover would have already allocated to the pool those aircraft that they wanted

Issue 7.

SPITFIRE & SEAFIRE

Identification : To identify individual marks, examine Form 700.

Engine :
Merlin : Spitfire I, II, IV, V, VI, VIIPR, VIIF, VIII, IX, X, XI, XIII, XVI.
Seafire I, II, III ....
Griffon : Spitfire XII, XIV, XVIII, XIX, 21, 22 ....
Seafire XV, 45 ....
Injection carb. on some Mks. indicated by wobble pump or booster pump switch.
No mixture lever except on early Mks.   Fuel : 100 Octane.

Supercharger : 2-speed, 2-stage type, with auto. control. Override switch on dash.
Keep UP for ferrying. Press button provided to ground test H.S. gear warning
light (Intercooler button must be IN). Some have 2-speed, single stage type,
with lever to pilot's left, fully back (M gear). A few have single-speed.

Propeller : Hydraulic constant speed.

Interconnected Throttle and Propeller Control (fitted to some) :
The prop. lever has two main positions. At AUTOMATIC, the throttle controls the
boost and revs. above 1800 r.p.m. At MAX. REVS., auto. device is overridden
and higher r.p.m. obtained. Most have manual range in between. Some have
Positive Coarse aft of gate (avoid selecting by mistake).

U/C Operation :
Normal :   Hydraulic. When raising or lowering U/C pause as soon as lever is
                out of notch. This allows weight of wheels to be lifted off locking
                pins. Then move lever to desired position at other end of quadrant,
                with a steady positive action and without pause. This is a safeguard
                against selector jamming. Lever will automatically spring into the
                other notch (Idle position). (Some Mk. I have hand pump with
                simple selector lever).
Reserve :   None.
Emergency : CO_2 cylinder. Selector must be DOWN. If selector jams midway
                apply negative " G " and bang it.
Indicator :   Green light, locked DOWN. Red light, locked UP. No lights
                IN TRANSIT. On some, stalks protruding above wings show
                position of each leg. Separate light for tail wheel (if retractable) :
                Green, locked DOWN. No warning horn.

Flaps :
Normal :   Compressed air. 2 or 3-position selector. No intermediate flap
                position.
Reserve :   None.
Emergency :   Spitfires : None.   Seafires : CO_2 bottle and control lever.
Indicators :   Bell cranks in wings.

Gills :
Manual control with single radiator. Auto. control with two radiators. Button
for ground testing. Some aircraft have carb. intake control to left of pilot.

(Continued overleaf

The ATA's Ferry Pilots Notes was the most comprehensive method of
recording the particulars of many different aircraft in one volume. Over
the next four pages the 'cards' pertinent to all different marks of Spitfires

SPITFIRE & SEAFIRE—*Continued.*

Main Tanks :
All aircraft have two main tanks in fuselage ; total capacity 85 or 96 gals. Contents gauge for lower main or for both. Early aircraft have a cock lever for each tank, others a single cock. Tanks are pressurised on most aircraft. Keep pressurising cock OFF. Booster or wobble pump fitted on those with injection carb. ; use in normal manner. Always take-off and land on Mains. For normal ferrying, long range tanks not used. Check empty as possible and keep their cocks OFF. Some Spitfire V have an immersed pump in lower tank with switch below rudder trimmer. Keep OFF for ferrying.

Long Range Tanks (sometimes fitted) :
Jettison : All except early aircraft can have 30, 45, 90 or 170 gal. tanks under fuselage. Cock lever and jettison hand grip to right of pilot. No gauge. Jettison the tank before belly landing or ditching. To do so check cock OFF and then pull hand grip.
75, 64, or 31-Gal. Rear Fuselage : Cock hand wheel near pilot's left knee. Single 3-position switch to left of pilot controls booster pump and also the main tank pump. Contents gauge.
29-Gal. Rear Fuselage : On some early aircraft. Cock to left of pilot. No booster pump and no gauge.
66-Gal. Leading Edge : Most P.R. aircraft have one in each wing. Cock levers to port. Usually a booster pump in each. The switches are with the main tank pump switch to right of pilot : sometimes replaced by a 3-position selector and ON-OFF switch. Gauge for each tank. Early aircraft have cocks on corresponding sides of cockpit (when not marked, ON fore-and-aft, OFF athwartships) and no booster pumps.
9, 14, or 18-Gal. Leading Edge : A few aircraft have one in each wing. Their contents transferred to top main tank by air pressure. Transfer cock below dash or to port. Only transfer when main tank level permits and keep main cock on. No gauges or booster pumps.
Contents Gauges : These vary even on same Mark depending on which tanks fitted. Examine labels closely to see to which tanks the gauges refer.
Method of Use : For long range work, where use is necessary, check contents visually before flight. Use one at a time when cruising in the order :— (1) Rear Fuselage. (2) Jettison. (3) 66-gal. leading edge (use evenly). Turn ON cock and booster pump of tank desired, before turning OFF tank in use. Only have one booster pump On at any one time. With full rear fuselage tank or with jettison tank fitted (full or empty), only normal ferrying manoeuvres permitted. Always take-off and land on main tanks.

Pressure Cabin :
There are two kinds. Some aircraft have a detachable hood which is lifted on after pilot is seated. Four cam levers must be forward. When hood is located, push levers back and connect two rubber tubes at sides. Keep cabin pressure control lever at left elbow, OFF. Two red lights show if it is ON. Automatic control may be fitted. To jettison, push forward two front levers and push hood upwards. Other aircraft have a sliding hood. Pressure lever to starboard and sealing cock to port must be OFF. To jettison, pull red knob on left dash and push hood upwards. On both types two air cocks by front windscreen panel must be OFF.

Folding Wings : On Seafire III and XV. When locked, indicator (small cylindrical block) is FLUSH with top surface of wing. Protrudes 1½″ when unlocked.

Starting : 12-volt or cartridge. With injection carb, Idle Cut-Off lever near throttle. If not fitted, pull out slow running ring control to get Idle Cut-Off.

Deck Arrester : Yellow T-handle to right rear. Green light, DOWN. To raise, push back FROM OUTSIDE.

Special Precautions : Propeller clearance is small and aircraft is nose heavy on ground. *With Merlin* : Two men on tail for run-up : do not exceed +6 boost unless specially moored. *With Griffon* : Tail anchored, run-up to +9 : do not exceed zero boost with tail unmoored.

(Continued on next card.

are shown. In these cards - accurate to Ammendment 25, dated 16/6/45 - 24 different aircraft sub-types are detailed. These four cards explain the differences in type, handling, operation of Flaps, Undercarriage,

Issue 7.

SPITFIRE & SEAFIRE—Continued.

FLYING PARTICULARS
Spitfires with MERLIN Engines

Take-Off :

					Trim :		
Booster Pump:	Boost :	R.P.M.:	Mix.:	Gills :	Elev.	Rudder :	Flaps
ON	Mk. I : +6¼.	3000.	Rich	Open	Neutral.	1 turn	UP.
(if fitted.)	Other		if		or	from	
	Mks. : +12.		fitted.		Auto.	either end.	

Climb (A.T.A.) :

Boost :	R.P.M. :	Booster Pump :	A.S.I. :
+6.	2600	OFF.	180 m.p.h.
	(2100 with prop.	(if fitted).	
	interconnected).		

A.T.A. Cruise :

Boost :	R.P.M.:	Mixture :	Gills :	A.S.I. :	Consumption :
0.	1900.	Weak if fitted.	Watch	195-215 m.p.h.	35-45 gals./hr.
(+1	1800.		temps.		

(with prop. interconnected).

Slow Flying :

Boost:	R.P.M.:	Mixture :	Gills :	Flaps :	A.S.I. :
As required.	2600 or Auto.	Rich if fitted.	Open or Auto.	DOWN.	120 m.p.h.

Stall :

	Flaps & U/C UP :	Flaps & U/C DOWN :
Mk. IV :	66 m.p.h.	56 m.p.h.
Mks. VIIF, VIII, IX, X, XI, XVI :	86 m.p.h.	76 m.p.h.
Other Marks :	70 m.p.h.	64 m.p.h.
Glide : Flaps & U/C UP :	110 m.p.h.	Flaps & U/C DOWN : 100 m.p.h.

Approach and Land :

Flaps :	Effect :	Max. speed for Flaps and U/C :	Final Approach :
DOWN.	Nose Down.	160 m.p.h.	Mk. IV : 80 m.p.h.
			Mks. VIIF, VIII, IX, X, XI, XVI : 90-95 m.p.h.
			Other Marks : 85 m.p.h.

Note : With jettison tanks, trim rudder FULL RIGHT for take-off. Add 5 m.p.h. to glide, stall and approach speeds if rear fuselage tank is full or jettison tank fitted. In Spitfire IV, oil tank is under pressure. Check that vent cock under port wing is closed before flight and opened after landing.

Seafires with MERLIN Engines

Take-Off :

				Trim :		
Boost :	R.P.M.:	Mixture :	Gills :	Elevator :	Rudder :	Flaps :
+12.	3000.	Rich if fitted.	Open.	Neutral.	1 turn from either end.	UP.

Climb (A.T.A.) :

Boost :	R.P.M.:		A.S.I.
+6.	2600.		160 knots.

A.T.A. Cruise :

Boost :	R.P.M.:	Mixture :	Gills :	A.S.I. :	Consumption :
0.	1900.	Weak if fitted.	Watch temps.	182 knots. (210 m.p.h.).	35-45 gals./hr.

Slow Flying :

Boost :	R.P.M.:	Mixture :	Gills :	Flaps :	A.S.I. :
As required.	2600.	Rich if fitted.	Open.	DOWN.	105 knots.

Stall : Flaps and U/C UP : 66 knots. Flaps and U/C DOWN : 56 knots.
Glide : Flaps and U/C UP : 87 knots. Flaps and U/C DOWN : 78 knots.

Approach and Land :

Flaps :	Effect :	Max. speed for Flaps and U/C :	Final Approach :
DOWN.	Nose Down.	140 knots.	75 knots.

Note : With jettison tanks, trim rudder FULL RIGHT for take-off and add 4 knots to glide, stall and approach speeds.

(Continued overleaf.

Radiator, Fuel system and other particulars. They also explain the differences in flying characteristics and the 'ATA Cruise' speeds that ferry pilots were to follow.

SPITFIRE & SEAFIRE—*Continued.*

FLYING PARTICULARS

Spitfires with GRIFFON Engines.

Take-Off :

Booster Pump :	Blower :	Boost :	R.P.M. :	Mixture :	Gills :	Elevator :	Trim : Rudder :
ON (if fitted.)	M.	+6 to +12 max.	2750.	None.	Open.	Neutral.	FULL LEFT.

Mk. XII : Only use +9 until U/C is up. [Flaps : UP.

Climb (A.T.A.) :

Boost :	R.P.M. :	Booster Pump :	A.S.I. :
+6.	2200 or AUTO.	OFF (if fitted).	180 m.p.h.

A.T.A. Cruise :

Boost :	R.P.M. :	Mixture :	Gills :	A.S.I. :	Consumption :
0˙	1800 or AUTO.	None.	Watch temps.	230-250 m.p.h.	60 gals./hr.

Slow Flying :

Boost :	R.P.M. :	Gills :	Flaps :	A.S.I. :
As required.	2400 or AUTO.	Open.	DOWN.	120-140 m.p.h.

Stall : Flaps and U/C UP : 88 m.p.h. Flaps and U/C DOWN : 75 m.p.h.

Glide : Flaps and U/C UP : 115 m.p.h. Flaps and U/C DOWN : 105 m.p.h.

Approach and Land :

Flaps :	Effect :	Max. speed for Flaps and U/C :	Final Approach :
DOWN.	Slight.	160 m.p.h.	100 m.p.h.

Note : With full rear fuselage tank or with jettison tanks, add 5 m.p.h. to glide, stall and approach speeds.

Seafires with GRIFFON Engines

Take-Off :

Blower :	Boost :	R.P.M. :	Mixture :	Gills :	Elevator :	Trim : Rudder :	Flaps :
M.	+6 to +12 max.	2750.	None.	Auto.	Neutral.	FULL LEFT.	UP.

Mk. XV : Only use +9 until U/C is up.

Climb (A.T.A.) :

Boost :	R.P.M. :	A.S.I. :
+6.	2200 or AUTO.	160 Kts.

A.T.A. Cruise :

Boost :	R.P.M. :	Mixture :	Gills :	A.S.I. :	Consumption :
0.	1800 or AUTO.	None.	Auto.	200 Kts. (230 m.p.h.).	60 gals./hr.

Slow Flying :

Boost :	R.P.M. :	Gills :	Flaps :	A.S.I. :
As required.	2400 or AUTO.	Auto.	DOWN.	105-120 Kts.

Stall : Flaps and U/C UP : 75 Kts. Flaps and U/C DOWN : 62 Kts.

Glide : Flaps and U/C UP : 100 Kts. Flaps and U/C DOWN : 90 Kts.

Approach and Land :

Flaps :	Effect :	Max. speed for Flaps & U/C :	Final Approach :
DOWN.	Slight.	140 Kts.	85 Kts.

The cards (reproduced actual size) covered everything from singled engined, light aircraft types to large, four engined bombers and transports moved, with their priority. The Operations Officer would make out a chit for each machine and allocate them according to those pilots available. Class I pilots would be given elementary trainers and light aircraft; Tiger Moths, Magisters, Proctors, Austers, Swordfish and the taxi Fairchilds. Class II - Spitfires, Hurricanes, Barracuda and any other single-engined aircraft, according to experience. Class III - the light twin engined aircraft; Oxfords, Dominies, and Avro Ansons, our taxi aircraft. Class IV - advanced twin engined machines: Hudsons, Wellingtons, Meteors etc and Class V - Four engined aircraft: Lancaster, Halifax etc, and of course anything else from the other classes. Operations Officers had a very responsible and not always easy job fitting in all the movements in co-operation with the other pools, arranging the taxi aircraft so as to bring their pilots back to base on the same day if at all possible. The taxi Fairchilds could take up to three pilots; four or more had to go in the Anson. This aircraft had been originally developed as a reconnaissance or bomber machine with a crew of five, but became the main taxi aircraft for ATA, carrying officially up to nine pilots and parachutes, but sometimes even ten or more!

The Anson was an easy aircraft to fly, its reliable Cheetah engines never seemed to go wrong and it appeared to float its own way down to the ground and land itself. The only awkward thing about it was the 120 turns of the hand-crank to raise or lower the undercarriage on those aircraft that did not have hydraulic gear, so an ATC cadet was often taken along to do the job, a task for which most of them contested with great enthusiasm.

The most important aircraft to be ferried were the ones from the factories or Maintenance Units (MUs). After these came the number of aircraft scattered around the countryside to be returned to their correct units or to be taken for repair, storage or breaking up.

CHAPTER FIVE
First Spitfire flights
and winter ferrying

Peggy, having completed her 50 hours taxi-ing and ferrying Class I aircraft in time to get onto the next Class II course at Thame, was sent there to find Joyce Fenwick and herself were the only two girls - the others on the course were RAF pilots seconded to ATA for ferrying duties. Their training was to be on Harvards; fast, exciting aircraft that were interesting to fly. The ground school was considerably more difficult: Carburettors, Superchargers and other accessories seemed to be much more complicated and there was so many of them to learn. Everyone was determined not to fail.

Peggy:
"With the flying I did not have much difficulty. I did have an Instructor who bellowed at me and reduced me to tears on more than one occasion, but I had my goggles on so he could not see them.

I nearly blotted my copybook on my first solo flight in a Harvard. The flap lever and undercarriage lever were close in this aircraft and in my excitement after the landing, I selected 'Undercarriage Up' instead of 'Flaps Up'. I realised my error immediately and tried to get the undercarriage lever back into its locked down position. As the weight of the aircraft was on it, this proved to be impossible and I did not dare taxi the aircraft in case the retractable undercarriage collapsed. Accordingly, I sat where I had finished my landing run until my instructor came out in a fury and asked me what I was doing. 'Don't tell me...' he said '... I know, you pulled the undercarriage lever!'. I nodded miserably. 'Stay there'.

He went to get the ground crew out. They had to get the aircraft jacked up on both sides before I could get the undercarriage locked down again so I could taxi in. I had, of course, to report to the Head of the School who tore me off a strip and told me I was extremely fortunate that I had not damaged the aircraft. I could not have agreed with him more heartily!

After a few hours solo in a Harvard, the final stage of training was a flight in a Spitfire. Like all single-seat fighters, it had to be flown solo from the word go, with no Instructor present to get the pilot out of trouble. Peggy continues:

"I sat in the Spitfire for quite an hour the day beforehand and familiarised myself with the cockpit controls and instruments. That night I went to bed early and read the handling notes at least 20 times. I never thought when joining the ATA that I would ever get to the stage of flying what to me was the most glamorous and graceful aircraft that I knew!

The next day, the weather was perfect; a blue sky with little white puffy cotton wool like clouds here and there. My Instructor gave me a short briefing and a few words of encouragement and then told me to take it away, fly it around a few turns to get the feel of it and then land back on the airfield.

I started up and taxied it down to the take-off point, doing everything very carefully and correctly and, upon getting a 'green' from the control opened up slowly and carefully to full throttle, watching the nose on the far hedge very intently in order to correct immediately the first signs of a swing. The surge of power as I opened up the throttle surprised me, but I was able to hold her straight and the take-off was smooth and effortless. I went through the normal procedure; undercarriage up, check to climbing speed and all the other items, climbing to 2,000 feet before turning. I could hardly believe it. I had realised one of my life's ambitions and was actually flying a Spitfire!

I thought 'I am going to make the most of this so that even if I crash it on landing, I will have known what it is like to fly'. I tried gentle turns and steeper turns; I climbed above a nice fluffy white cloud, throttled back, held the nose up and let it stall. The stall was surprisingly gentle, and only by my rapid descent to the cloud below did I realise it, to start with. I enjoyed the day, the clouds and the aircraft. Its small cockpit seemed to be built right around one and it was almost as though one had wings oneself. 'This is flying...' I thought ' ... and I should never get tired of flying this machine under these conditions'

Gradually it dawned on me that perhaps I was staying up longer than i should. I looked around for the airfield and I saw it some distance away, so I flew back and made a very correct approach and landing. Thame was rather a small airfield, therefore there was not much spare landing room. I was very relieved when I touched down reasonably close to the boundary and had the whole length of the airfield in which to pull up. I taxied in, switched off and climbed out of the plane, feeling very pleased with myself - only to be met by my rather irate Instructor, who ticked me off for being so long and leaving the circuit. I was completely honest with him. I told him that I was determined to make the most of my first Spitfire flight in case it was my last! He laughed and all was well.

Joyce Fenwick

Joyce Fenwick was not so lucky. She had the misfortune to drop a Harvard rather heavily during a training flight. This was considered dangerous and also damaged the machine, so poor Joyce was taken off her Class II course and sent back to ferry Class I aircraft. The repercussions of this affected me. The CO of the Thame Ferry Pool sent for

me and told me that as winter was approaching it had been decided that I should also be put back to ferrying only Class I aircraft until the spring. I asked whether this was to apply to all RAF pilots on the course and was told 'No, it did not'. I pointed out that both in Ground tests and practical Flying my reports had been quite as good as any of theirs - in fact, better than some - and I considered this a completely unjust action which was made only because I was a woman. Captain Hill replied 'There is nothing you can do about it, the decision has been made'.

I was not going to give up my Spitfires without a fight. I said to him 'With all due respect Sir, there is something I can do about it. I can leave the ATA and return to my duties as a WAAF Officer'. He said 'You wouldn't be so foolish'. I replied it was a matter of opinion as to what actions were foolish. It might be considered foolish by some to waste the Government's money in training a pilot to ferry Spitfires and other Class II aircraft and then not allow them to do so!

I left his office in a fuming rage and could think of nothing and no-one to take it out on. At lunch my RAF colleagues were sympathetic but unhelpful.

After lunch I was surprised to hear my name called over the Tannoy to report to flying control. I was to fly as passenger to White Waltham with Lois Butler to see Pauline Gower herself and the Head of ATA, Gerard d'Erlanger.

During the flight I wondered what I had let myself in for, and what I was going to say. I went rather nervously into Miss Gower's office and felt myself being carefully scrutinised by her keen blue eyes. She asked me to explain the situation and listened to my point of view, I thought, with a certain amount of sympathy. I think she had had much tougher fights than this over the same sort of thing during the early days. She made no comment but sent me to see Gerard d'Erlanger, who tried to persuade me that it was for my own good to fly the easier aircraft during the winter. I replied that on joining the ATA we had been told that we could expect no consideration because we were women and accordingly I saw no reason why my good should be considered more than that of the other RAF pilots on the same course. I said I felt I was being victimised because I was a woman. I thought to myself secretly that 'victimised' was rather a good word. He told me to wait and he would talk to Miss Gower.

A few minutes later I was called back and told that they did not want me to feel that there was any victimisation or unfairness and that if my flying reports from Thame were up to the same standard as those of the men, I could go ahead and ferry Class II aircraft.

I flew back with Lois Butler, very please at having won my first battle. Lois was one of the oldest women pilots in ATA - in fact one of the first to get a licence before the war. She did not say much, but from the twinkle in her eye I could see that she approved. She was the wife of the Chairman of De Havilland's, which is why she learned to fly so early on. Carol, her daughter used to be very embarrassed when her mother would fly down to Roedean for Speech day or some such occasion and land on the playing field. No other mother was so 'way out' and she hated it, according to June who was a great friend of hers.

We had a Ferry Training Pool at Thame, and to this I was now posted for a limited amount of ferrying, as were all the new pilots, until I got my posting to another pool. I was the only one from the original WAAF here at first. The winter was now approaching and the weather starting to get more uncertain. To start with we did a lot of waiting around for the weather and took to playing bridge while we did so. I had a few aircraft to ferry, but mostly Class I machines, Tiger Moths, Proctors, Swordfish and the like. At last one day I collected my chit from Operations and saw that I had a Spitfire to collect from North Weald. I had never visited this famous fighter station and was dropped there in the taxi aircraft, feeling rather thrilled at collecting my first operational aircraft. I found that it was not ready

Ready to go! Diana Faunthorpe and 'Pooh' Stokes in full flying kit at
Barton-in-the-Clay

for me, as it had not yet had a daily inspection. It had been parked away in the hangar for some days as it did not belong to a North Weald squadron, but had been left there for repair by another squadron's pilot. It was suggested that I should go to the Mess for an early lunch and by the time I had finished it would be ready. I found it very satisfying, when asked by various pilots what I was there for to be able to reply 'I'm collecting a Spit'.

After lunch I got into the aircraft and taxied it down to the end of the runway for take-off. I opened up steadily to full throttle and had covered about four hundred yards when it suddenly swung off the runway to the right, and did not respond to anything I tried to do to control the swing, but came to a sudden stop in the soft mud at the side of the runway and tipped onto its nose. It was a good thing no-one was around to hear my language! I cursed myself with just about every word I knew, and thought to myself 'you bloody fool, so much for thinking that you could ferry aircraft of this type in winter. Now they will be able to say that they knew this would happen'. I looked around for the crash tender, but there was no movement on the airfield. I undid my harness and, having switched everything off rather belatedly, clambered out of the cockpit. I found getting to the ground rather difficult. I no longer had a wing to stand on and was amazed how far off the ground the cockpit was when the aircraft was standing on its nose!

I threw out my overnight bag and parachute, then dropped to the ground, my feet squelching in the mud alongside them. I looked at the aircraft; my beautiful Spitfire had the blades of its metal propeller curled back like the petals on a dying daisy. And I had done that. I could hardly believe it and could not understand how, but there it was. I looked around the airfield again but no-one appeared to be noticing my existence. Control must have seen me I thought, but nobody came, so I stood there thinking about how I would write out the accident report and wondering what to do next. Suddenly the control van from the end of the runway started up the runway in my direction. It stopped when it got level with the plane and an officer got out and came towards me. I picked up my belongings and went over to meet him. He apologised that the crash tender was not available, apparently it refused to start!. He said he had been unable to come until control had given him permission, but as both he and control had seen me get out, they could see that I was alright. I climbed into the van and we started driving back down the runway.

'Damn bad luck a tyre bursting on take-off like that' he said. I stopped breathing. So that was it, and it was not my fault!. I tried to look unconcerned. 'Look, there are the pieces of the tyre and some metal from the wheel hub' 'Could we stop for a moment?' I asked. He pulled up and I picked up the couple of chunks of metal. With the wheel hub broken nobody could expect any pilot to keep the aircraft on the runway at speed. I looked lovingly at the little bits of metal and thought 'this little bit of evidence I am going to keep'. I looked back at the aircraft. On the side that I had not got out, the wheel, or what was left of it was buried deep in the mud. I had not even noticed that anything was wrong, because you could not see it! The ground was very soft there and the wheels had sunk in very deeply.

We drove round to the Engineers Office; he was full of apology. He said 'We had just repaired a puncture in that tyre. It was one of those borderline cases, but we decided that a repair was justified rather than a replacement. It seems we were wrong. Now it will have to have a new prop - a new tyre and tube would have been easier'.

I went to flying control and rang up my ferry pool. I told them 'I had a tyre burst on take-off and I already had too much speed up and was unable to stop it swinging off the runway and nosing over'. They said they would send a taxi-plane in about an hour.

I had plenty of time to write my accident report and draw the sketch. I omitted to say however, that I had no idea at all as to what had happened until an RAF officer had told me! I returned to my pool, presented my accident report and my two little pieces of metal as evidence.

Accidents were classed in a number of categories: Pilot to blame - an accident that was entirely due to an error or bad airmanship on the part of the pilot; Pilot responsible - where the accident was not entirely the pilot's fault, but possibly could have been prevented. Pilot not responsible - where an accident was due to mechanical or other defect beyond the pilot's control. Unless one had a very good record, an accident or two where the pilot was to blame would probably mean dismissal from the ATA.

Naturally, I was vastly relieved when in my case the comment was 'Pilot not responsible'. After this inauspicious start to my Spitfire ferrying, I was fortunately able to move the next ones I was given in one piece and without incident".

In November, Suzanne started Class II training, which was interupted over Christmas - nevertheless, she flew the Spitfire on 11th January, a nice start to a new year.

In winter the weather often made flying without radio difficult or impossible. Class II training at Thame stopped, allowing the Instructors to have their annual leave over Christmas, as grass airfields often became very wet and were often declared unserviceable. Peggy was lucky to complete her Class II before November: most of the others had to wait, continuing to ferry Class I aircraft until the next course started in February.

June, with her artistic sense and observation, noticed how, when the snow had fallen lightly, it would outline one side of the hedgerow only, and put the trees and buildings into stark relief. When shadows grew long in the evening, trees and woods looked unreal in their beauty. When the snow was actually falling, it was not so good; with no windscreen wipers one could see nothing and if one met snowstorms the wisest thing to do was to turn around and go back to the nearest airfield.

Several times the weather made overnight stops unavoidable - we woke up to a white world in the morning and were stuck until the runways were cleared. This might take an hour or two, or several days, depending on how much had fallen and what the facilities for clearance were. Peggy, having been stuck at a temporarily disused airfield that was manned by only a skeleton staff had the runway flattened for her by a gang of 'glasshouse' inmates - occupants of the RAF Punishment centre - they had to run up and down the runway in formation until the snow was hard!

'I felt awful watching them, it must have been exhausting, but it did the trick. I had a firm enough runway to take off from, even if it was somewhat uneven!'

The pilots only had small overnight bags, which already contained maps and ferry Pilots Notes, so there was not much room left for extra clothing for a prolonged stay.

Sue Alexander and Pat Provis were posted up to Prestwick for a month; they both had trouble with Swordfish there. The Swordfish was a very large single engined bi-plane that was still used operationally by the Fleet Air Arm at the beginning of the war, but now, in 1943 the type was normally only used for training or experimental purposes. Many had came to the end of their useful lives and were being ferried for storage or breaking up.

Sue, conscientious and competent, taking her first one, took the booklet of the complete handling notes of the aircraft with her and, on looking up the details for landing found the instruction 'release bungy control'

"I could not understand what it meant and kept circling the airfield trying to work out what it was, getting repeated greens from Control until eventually I hoped that it was not vital and landed. My handling notes looked much the worse for wear and the groundstaff thought it was quite funny at the time".

If she had looked in her little blue book on the Swordfish card she would have seen that it was an elastic cord used to bias the rudder and controlled by a knob at the pilot's right hand - 'The pull of the cord is very powerful and should be slackened off before landing' (to prevent swing when power is reduced). Hard to find in a hurry in the complete handling booklet, but instantly to hand in the little blue book.

Another time she found herself snowed up in Lossiemouth for a considerable period and spent the time 'playing poker with a lot of rather elderly male pilots, equally snowed up'. Finally the snow was piled into a wall either side of the runway and she decided she could take-off:

"I failed to prevent the Swordfish from swinging and ploughed into the snow bank. When it struck, I cut the engine and switched off the petrol as the plane calmly somersaulted onto its back. There I was, upside down with nothing on the clock! As my head was quite a long way above the concrete runway I decided to await help, which came in the form of a fire-engine and crash tender. Feeling rather foolish, but also inclined to giggle, I had to report to the Co of the Lossiemouth pool who, I gathered did not approve of women pilots, and no doubt was confirmed in that opinion!. I fear it went down on my record as 'pilot error'. The Swordfish was an old one, going to be broken up, but they did not want it broken up on their runway!"

Pat Provis, fair-haired, attractive, with a lovely sense of humour also had Swordfish trouble at Prestwick...
"The petrol pump packed up when I was close to Turnberry airfield. I thought the forced-landing would be easy, but made a horrible mess of it and finished up on the sea wall - what is now I think the 9th hole on Turnberry Golf Course. You will remember that the most dangerous thing about a Swordfish was the climbing in and out of it. However, on this occasion that was no problem, I just put my foot over the side and there was the ground. I was still more or less on the airfield, so the fire engine and Ambulance came out pretty smartly but not before the Station Engineering Officer, who rushed up and asked 'Where's the Form 700, and, by the way, are you all right?' Then somebody said, 'Christ, it's a woman!'. I replied 'Yes, it's a woman, so can you see if you can find me a mirror?' There was some discussion as to whether I had broken my nose, but I managed to convince them it was just that sort of nose. They then took me in the Ambulance to the Sick Quarters where they gave me the very latest treatment for crashed pilots - a cup of tea and two Aspirins".

Barbara took an Auster into Manston:
"...impossibly strong wind, 90° to the runway and fighters coming in right, left and centre made me decide to land on the grass. My aircraft was swarmed over when reaching the tarmac. 'Was I alright and was the aircraft alright?' Seems that the guns of a Spitfire were being tested and I had taxied right across the line of fire!. That was a horrible unwelcoming place, and, to me, an extreme example of the frustrations of our radio-less flying. The Tower felt the same I am sure".

Katie:
"Flying a Tiger Moth from Thame to Prestwick, I made a landing at Hawarden to re-fuel. When taxi-ing back for take-off I opted for the paved taxi-track. I did not realise that a Lancaster, with tail towards the track had its engines running. When I got behind it, the prop-wash flipped me over onto my nose. So much for Prestwick that day!"

Katie on the wing of a Hurricane

June, incidentally, the shortest pilot in the ATA was stuck out at Hawarden over the New Year by fog...

"It was a refit station for aircrew who needed to make up a new team for bombers. I landed there in my little Tiger Moth and was stuck there for three days over the New Year. I was adopted by a Wellington crew who had lost their skipper. It was a highly emotional and marvellous time for one lived for the moment and discounted the lives lost. These wonderful kids made me their skipper for that short duration and we did everything as a team; Church on Sunday, parties, the lot. It was desperately sad, they did not last long when back on Ops - but such was life - one had to cope with that and one did".

All the girls enjoyed the fact of being alive. Deaths of friends always came as a shock, but they tried not to feel guilty to be survivors. Most lost someone they knew well during the war. They tried not to react badly to disaster, and in time learnt to resist it. Husbands, brothers, cousins and RAF boyfriends; unforgettable comrades for a short time in the middle of a world war. Still, romance played its part. Frankie, Katie and Joyce all married whilst in ATA. Rosemary and Peggy had both lost pilot husbands. Frankie's husband nearly died in an air crash in Scotland.

One automatically had an affinity with other pilots; the higher one climbs in an aircraft, the smaller and less important things appear on the ground. One gains a new perspective. Every pilot has experienced this, and shares this non-transferable experience with other pilots; apart from the fact that the RAF pilots were our heroes and the reason for the ATA's existence.

In the previous April the intake had been joined by a most unusual recruit, not, however, from the WAAF. Coming home from Barton one evening they had found a very beautiful girl in their sitting room, busy ironing her underwear. Shiela Garrett had just arrived from the USA where she had been teaching flying, a fact they found very hard to believe. Sheila had been a top model in New

York, and a leading girl in 'Goldwin's Follies - A Pretty Girl is like a Melody'. Blonde, long-legged, she had intelligence, determination, sensibility and a strong sense of moral commitment. She had married and divorced an English film actor and had used her so-acquired British Passport and nationality to leave the USA to come over and take a more active part in the war. She joined the girls at Barton as she had to go through the same training but, of course, in no time she was on Proctors at Thame and then on Cross Country Flight, passing every test easily on account of her previous ability and experience.

She proved an excellent and level-headed friend to the ex-WAAF pilots, giving advice whenever asked, and telling what was in store next. Generous in every way and liked by all she astounded the men, who as one mechanic put it whilst sadly shaking his head 'I don't believe anyone looking like that could possibly fly an aircraft - she's Jane with her clothes on!' 'Jane' of course, was a cartoon figure in the 'Daily Mirror', usually loosing her clothes!

Sheila said to one of the girls who was upset when her RAF boyfriend had been killed:

"It will probably be you and me one day, but the great advantage of flying is that it is usually quick. One blinding flash and then unconsciousness. Much better than having an arm or a leg blown off by a bomb. I think civilians have a lot more to face in the war than pilots have".

When she finished Class II she was posted down to Hamble, together with Mary and Monique, who had come from the RAF Nursing Service and were one course ahead.

Peggy:
"The idea of an all-women's pool seemed pretty grim to both Shiela and myself and I expressed my sympathy. However, she rang me up after a few days and said it was quite different from what she had expected. The CO was

was quite different from what she had expected. The CO was marvellous, it was a nice area and there seemed to be possibilities of getting cottages to live in in the area, as most others had. Later she told me that she had found a lovely little place, an expensively converted weekend cottage from pre-war yachting days at Old Bursledon, and that she was already sharing this with Monique Agazarian and Mary Guthrie, both of whom I knew well from Thame as they were doing their Class II conversion course when I was on Cross Country Flight. She suggested that after I had finished at Thame I should apply for a posting there too.

Meanwhile I continued at the Thame Ferry Pool. Ferrying aircraft in winter had its disadvantages, mainly on account of the weather, but it was never boring. There were always plenty of aircraft to be moved from place to place and one never knew when one visited operations in the morning where one was going to get to and where one would finish that evening. On one occasion I was allocated a Proctor which had to go to Kirkbride on the Scottish border. I went to Met. There was fog up the East Coast and bad weather coming slowly in from the West, but there seemed a reasonable chance of getting through. I got up as far as Lancashire without trouble and then found the cloud very low. I decided to follow the coast round as there were several airfields conveniently placed where one could land if it got too bad. Finally, the cloud was right down and I had to turn back and land at Barrow-in-Furness, which I had previously passed over. The next morning the weather was still bad, but had cleared by lunchtime.

Taxi-ing out for take-off I head a bang and the aircraft slewed to the left. This time I knew what it was - a burst tyre. I switched off and walked through the wet puddles to Control. The mechanics brought the aircraft in and removed the tyre. It was quite irreparable. A search through the stores revealed that there was no spare Proctor tyre on the station. We rang around several other size. I rang the ferry pool and asked for instructions. They told me to wait with the aircraft and they would arrange for a tyre to be sent from Manchester the next day. Another night in Barrow-in-Furness, which, as far as I could find, had nothing to offer me apart from wet feet, in winter, in wartime.

I hung around Flying Control all the next day, but no tyre arrived. Finally, in the evening, a message came through that the aircraft bringing me the tyre had landed en route with engine trouble.

The tyre finally arrived the next day, after lunch. By the time that it was fixed on and the machine was signed out, I had only 20 minutes of daylight left, so I could no longer take-off.

The next day, the weather was bad. By this time I had developed a hearty dislike of Barrow-in-Furness. We always carried a small overnight bag with us, with a clean shirt and toilet things, but it was never sufficient for a stay of three or four days, especially when a lot of the time it was pouring with rain and no transport available. One had continual wet feet and no change of shoes! Finally the weather improved slightly and I got away after lunch the following day and thankfully delivered my Proctor to Kirkbride. Another front was coming in and Kirkbride was very doubtful about any aircraft doing much flying the next day. They suggested I stayed the night and possibly get a lift as far as Manchester in the morning. As it seemed doubtful, and I had had enough of being 'stuck out', I decided to catch the night train down. We were issued with travel warrants so that we could always return to our pool by train if necessary.

I arrived in London very early in the morning, caught a train back to Aylesbury and got a lift to the airfield. I had a quick wash, collected a clean shirt and reported to operations. I was instantly given a chit, an Auster from Aston Down to Kirkbride!

The taxi aircraft was leaving immediately, so I had no time to do anything except collect a bar of chocolate which was issued to us as an emergency ration in case we had to forgo lunch, collect the handling notes for the Auster as I had not flown one before, and go off.

At Aston Down there were a number of Maintenance Units. I went to the one designated, but they had never heard of my Auster - they had no Austers at all. They suggested another MU across the airfield. I went across - same story. I trudged to each MU in turn, but they all denied knowledge of my Auster. I rang back to my pool. They checked with Ferry Command in Andover. They rang me back, they said it must be at the first MU. I went back again. There was a consultation. Another engineer was called in and he said 'Oh yes, there is an Auster at the back of one of the hangars. It's been there for months and has never been flown'. After checking through numerous books and logs it was discovered that the aircraft had been left there by a Group Captain some months before and had obviously been forgotten. It was dug out from the back of the hangar, cleaned and inspected.

This was obviously going to take some time, so I went across to our ferry pool there and had lunch. Finally, it was ready for me. I got in and followed the starting procedure according to the book without result. The mechanics shook their head pityingly as if to say 'Women Pilots, what can you expect?'. Eventually I gave up and let them have a go. They tried everything, but it still would not start. 'It started perfectly on test just before' they said. The mechanics took out the plugs, dried and cleaned them and did everything else they could think off, but to no avail. The engineer tried again, but the engine obstinately refused to do anything. I got in again, tried a few times, gave it much more throttle than recommended and it suddenly sprang into life with a terrific roar, causing the mechanic who swung the prop to jump back hastily.

It was now pretty late, and it was clear that I could not reach Kirkbride that night. I decided to push on as far as I could. It was getting dark as I approached Cranage in Cheshire. This was an RAF training school I had visited once before; they had accomodation for WAAF, so it would be a good place to stop for the night. I landed the little Auster and was surprised at the very short landing run after the faster aircraft I had been flying. It was put away for the night. The next morning the entire airfield was covered in about three inches of snow. It was declared unserviceable and I had to wait another day until they had cleared the runways and markers.

Next morning the Auster started first swing and I set course against a strong North-East wind for Kirkbride. The Auster was a slow aircraft and, against the wind the traffic on the roads below seemed to be going faster! In addition, patches of low cloud started to appear. Forecasts had been clear around the coast, so I decided to go that way, but realised I would be rather short of petrol at my present groundspeed and so I looked for a suitable airfield to re-fuel and check the weather. It would not be Barrow-in-Furness!

A Fleet Air Arm station looked inviting and so I landed and re-fuelled. The Auster would not start again! Once again, the 'Woman Pilot' look appeared on the faces of the naval mechanics. Finally, an Engineering Officer asked if he could try. He had no luck either. Out came the plugs again and everything was tried. (Years later, having found out that some Austers with Lycoming engines would start easily when hot or cold but were tricky when warm, an Austrian Mechanic at Linz pointed out the cause and corrected it, after both the aircraft and engine manufacturers had been unable to account for the cause).

Meanwhile, the Fleet Air Arm struggled all afternoon. A weather check showed that Kirkbride was closed due to low cloud, so there was no point in going on that night. The WRENS put me up in their Nissen hut, where they made me feel like an honoured guest, putting flowers, Elizabeth Arden toilet soap and a guest towel in my room.

Next morning, visability was good, the Auster started first go and I flew up the Cumberland coast on the lee of Shapfell in a very strong North-East wind. The Auster started to loose height very rapidly, in spite of the increased throttle, teaching me a lesson on the down-draughts to be expected on the lee sides of mountains in strong winds. Moving a little further out from the coast improved the situation, but it was one of the bumpiest flights I had ever experienced. On arrival at Kirkbride there was again no aircraft going south, so I took the train back for a second time".

June:
"Talking of train journeys, do you recall that one was guaranteed a sleeper, providing one booked in through Ops before 3pm, often displacing a senior ranking type who would not find that he had lost his bunk until he arrived at the train. Not a happy man! And how, as aircrew one was always eligible for an egg for breakfast at RAF stations; so on principal one always took it as there was always some eager person who would eat it"

Peggy was given a Lysander for the first time...
"It was a very short delivery flight so, as it was a cabin aircraft. I did not take flying boots or heavy flying kit. On landing at the delivery station they did not want it and told me to take it to another unit further north. This place did not want it either and, after phone calls to my pool and Ferry Command at Andover, they told me to take it to a third place, from where I could bring a Magister back to an airfield not far from my pool, who would pick me up there. This sounded alright and I delivered my Lysander and collected my Maggie, only to realise on climbing into the cockpit that I had no outer flying clothing and of course, it was an open cockpit! As the flight was only a short one, and the alternative was to be stuck out for the night, I decided to take it. I froze! I had never realised how cold

73

one could get in an open cockpit in Winter, even on a short flight. When I landed I could hardly climb out of the aircraft I was so numb. Flying Control produced a hot cup of tea, however, and let me thaw out with them whilst waiting for the taxi aircraft".

CHAPTER SIX
Ferrying from Hamble

The ATA provided an important link between the factories and the RAF and FAA. They collected aircraft from the factories and took them to the Maintenance Units where they were fitted with wireless, guns, long-range tanks or any other items of specialised equipment according to what they were going to do. The ATA then collected them again and took the aircraft on to the RAF or FAA, often bringing back old ones for repair or breaking up. It was quite usual to fly two, three or even four different types in a day. The training was built up gradually to fly more advanced types, until the highest level was reached and any type could be flown. During the war there were over one hundred different types in production and some of the senior pilots had flown most of them. If the distances were long, pilots often took them to other Ferry Pools for onward ferrying, ie, Kirkbride for Scotland etc to save pilots from being away too long from their home base.

Peggy:
"In February I was sent down to Hamble. I rang up Sheila and she instantly said that I must join her and Mary and Monique in their cottage. I found everything exactly as she described it. In spite of being a pool run and staffed entirely by women, (except the mechanics and engineers) it was amazingly successful. The CO, Margot Gore was quite an exceptional person. She had an extremely logical mind, was very fair in all her judgements and was respected by everyone, male and female. She herself was fully qualified on all aircraft with the exception of flying boats, which no women flew. The cottage at Bursledon was a dream. It was two old cottages knocked into one, and upstairs had four bedrooms and two bathrooms. Down below was a large

sitting room with open fireplace and a very modern kitchen. We took it in turns by the month to do the house-keeping and it all worked out very well. We found a daily woman to come and clean for us and any necessary shopping we did on our way to and from the airfield. Both Mary and I had cars, for which we were allowed a limited petrol ration for commuting to the airfield. In practice we usually all four went in one car and in this way saved up a bit of petrol, which we had spare when we wanted to drive anywhere on leave.

The ferrying from Hamble was interesting. We had a lot of Spitfires off the field, which had to be taken to Maintenance Units for further equipment. We also cleared some of the factories assembling aircraft locally; Barracudas from Eastleigh, Fireflies, Mustangs and Typhoons from other airfields in the area".

Katie:
"While seconded to Hamble I once had to fly very low because of the weather. I was afraid I'd overshot my destination, so when I saw an airfield I landed to find out where I was. I discovered that my airfield was just over the next hill, so I hopped back in my Auster and took off, not bothering to fasten my seat-belt. I had not realised how bumpy it was, and there I was, bouncing around, hitting my head on the roof, unable to take my hands off the stick to do up my seat-belt. I never did that again".

Peggy:
'My first flight in a Barracuda I shall not easily forget. I had to take one from Worthy Down up to a Fleet Air Arm Station in Scotland, from where I had another aircraft back again. I read up the notes on the Barracuda. Margot told me beforehand a bit about what it was like and said it was an easy aircraft to fly once you were used to the pilot's seat being a long way off the ground. When I came to climb into the aircraft, I realised how true this was. I belive the Fleet Air Arm had in many cases specially

A good way of demonstrating the size of a Barracuda that shows why ladders were needed! Henry Arthur (above) and Pooh Stokes (below) pose alongside the aircraft coded '8K'

constructed ladders for the pilot to reach his seat. Otherwise it was a sort of mountaineering feat, with hand and foot-holds up the undercarriage to reach the cockpit. There was room in the belly of the machine for an observer, but he was cut off from the pilot completely, except for a very small space where he could glance up into the cockpit. There was no intercom fitted yet.

I was sitting in the aircraft checking to see where everything was, when two naval officers approached me. One of them climbed up to the cockpit and I saw he was a Fleet Air Arm pilot. He told me that both of them had got leave and that their home was in Scotland. They had permission to fly with me if I would take them as passengers. I told them that I was not at all keen on taking any passengers as I had not flown a Barracuda before and would not, in any case, be taking off for at least half an hour as I wanted to familiarise myself with the strange type before taking it into the air. I suggested that they went round and tried to find another aircraft.

In about 20 minutes they were back again. There was no-one else going. It was an ideal opportunity for them; by train it would mean an extra day off their leave. Please could I take them? Very reluctantly, I agreed. They both climbed into the observer's seat and, when I was ready, we took off. I decided to make a half-way stop to refuel and when I got to the circuit, I joined it and then got out my little book "Ferry Pilots Notes" to check how many degrees of flap I should use on the approach. I came into land very carefully, remembering that my wheels were much lower beneath me than in a normal fighter aircraft. I managed to make a quite reasonable landing and taxied to control and got out. I asked my passengers how they were and they said 'Fine, but we were a little bit worried when we saw you reading a book going around the circuit! Do you always do that sort of thing?'. I explained that it was, in fact, quite a frequent practice amongst us when flying strange types as it was not always possible to keep everything in ones head and it was much better to check and be sure!

On another occasion I had a Martinet to take down to Cornwall to one of the coastal stations for target towing. It was a lovely day and I was just enjoying the beauty of the Devon countryside from the air when there was the most horrible crack. It sounded exactly as though a main spar had broken. My heart leapt into my mouth and I looked hastily around; everything appeared normal and I could not think of anything it could be. Shortly afterwards there was another. I tested all the controls gingerly - everything seemed alright. I was flying over heavily wooded country with no airfield close by, so I thought the best thing to do was to carry on. Nothing further happened.

When I arrived at St Eval, I joined the circuit and got a green light. I started my approach and was rather taken aback to see an ambulance and the crash tender racing towards the runway. I looked behind and saw a Liberator.

Thinking he must be in trouble, perhaps even with wounded aboard, I opened the throttle and went round again, leaving the approach free for him. On the downwind leg of the circuit I saw that he had gone off in another direction and that the ambulance and fire tender had moved back to the end of the runway again. I was given another green. I made another approach. As I passed over the end of the runway, the fire tender and ambulance accompanied me, one on each side of the grass. This shook me to the core. I came to the conclusion that I perhaps had only one undercarriage leg down.

The Martinet however, had a practically foolproof mechanical indicator system and this showed the undercarriage in the 'down and locked' position. I flew low the full length of the runway, turning slightly to look at my own shadow. As far as I could see I had two wheels. I again climbed up and went round the circuit. The ambulance and fire tender returned and positioned themselves on the approach end of the runway again. I looked round for the Liberator, or any other aircraft, thinking that it could not be me, but there was no other aircraft in sight. I approached again and this time made a careful landing, still accompanied by the ambulance and fire tender. I taxied in and they returned to their normal position by Control.

I got out of the aircraft and as I jumped to the ground I saw the cause   of the excitement. The fabric of the machine had peeled off the underside from the cowling right back to the tail where it was still firmly attached. Two large strips of canvas must have been flapping wildly behind the plane, and they were probably afraid that it had fouled the rudder or elevator. In point of fact it had done neither, and, as far as I could see, had not affected the flying characteristics of the aircraft in the slightest. Inspection of the log-book revealed that it had just been repaired after a previous crash and the fabric underneath was new and obviously had not been attached properly.

I had been told that I would have to find my own way back from this flight as it was too far to send a taxi aircraft specially to fetch me. I rang Bristol, the nearest Ferry Pool, but they had nothing going in my direction. I asked the Station if they had anything that I could get a lift with and was told 'We have a Spitfire here which should go to Aston Down. We would be very glad if you would take that'. It was brought out and serviced and I flew it to start with to our Ferry Pool at Whitchurch Airfield, Bristol. I thought that as it was in their area I had better check with them. In any case, they might like to take it to Aston Down and I could get a train more easily from Bristol. They, however, refused to have anything to do with it as it was not on their books, so I flew it to Aston Down. Once again, they refused to accept it.

After much telephoning, they told me 'This aircraft no longer exists. it was marked off as crashed in France some six months ago'. Now, at St Eval they had told me that the aircraft had been left there by a pilot who had stolen it off a German airfield in France and he had used it to escape to England. No Maintenance Unit would accept the papers. 'What shall I do with it?' I asked one Officer. He said to me 'If I were you, I would land it in someone's private park and hide it away under some trees. You will find at the end of the war you will own a Spitfire! Once anything has been 'written off ' in the RAF it literally no longer exists for them'.

It was almost a temptation to do as he said, but I felt it might be useful again and I must do something with it. As Andover was much nearer to my base, I decided to fly it to Ferry Command there and leave them to deal with the problem. This I did and was rather relieved when they accepted the papers without question. I was beginning to feel rather guilty that I had accepted the aircraft without having any authorisation".

When pilot's were given their instructions from Operations in the morning they usually had black and white forms with details of the aircraft to be collected and where it had to go. If the aircraft was required urgently, it was given a blue form marked *'Priority Two'* ; if its delivery was very urgent indeed with red , marked *'Priority One'* . With 'Priority One' aircraft, the instructions were to get the aircraft through with the least delay compatible with the pilot's ability. Only reliable and experienced pilots were issued with Priority Ones. Peggy had never had one of these and was very surprised when Alision, the Hamble Operations Officer said 'I have a red chit for you this morning'. It was a Swordfish to be collected from a Naval Air Station on the Fifeshire coast and to be delivered to Worthy Down in Hampshire. She could not think why a Swordfish could possibly be 'Priority One', but apparently there was a ship waiting for it to go to the Far East.

'I had a Barracuda to deliver up there, and then this Swordfish back. The weather was bad, and showed signs of deteriorating on the way up. When I went to get the Swordfish, they gave me another chit to say that this aircraft must have a guard on it at all times as it had secret equipment fitted. When it was wheeled out of the hangar the mechanic said 'Looks like a Christmas tree don't it!'. It was all white and covered with all sorts of strange bulges in unusual places. The Met office was not encouraging; the whole of the East coast was by now covered by a widespread front with low cloud and the only possibility of getting the aircraft through to the South would be towards the West. In view of the priority I decided to attempt it and crossed to the West coast and down to Lancashire OK, then the cloud became very low. I kept to the low ground and made several attempts to get towards the East, but in every case I had to turn back as the cloud came down to the ground. The only possibility was South-westwards where the cloud-base was slightly higher.
    At Worcester there was still no gap anywhere in the clouds and I was forced to stay below them. Going up

through the cloud with no radio would only have led to worse trouble; there would probably never be a gap to come down in again. This was how Amy Johnson met her death and I did not want to put myself in the same position. I had a strong southerly wind against me and the Swordfish, never a fast aircraft, seemed to crawl along the ground incredibly slowly. I realised that at this slow speed I would soon be running out of daylight; with luck I might reach our Ferry Pool at Bristol. This however, was not possible as already north of Bristol the cloud was right down. I turned back to an aerodrome near Cheltenham and circled it. There was no aircraft to be seen in the air or on the ground but I got a welcoming green light from Flying Control, landed and taxied in. I showed them the papers and explained my position. The Control Officer threw up his eyes in horror when he saw the bits about having to have a guard on it. He said that the hangars were all completely full and the aircraft would have to remain picketed outside all night with some poor unfortunate body detailed to guard it! There was no possibility of getting to another airfield as by this time it was already dusk, so I saw the aircraft firmly tied down, facing the wind, and went to enquire about the weather possibilities the next day. There was no Met Office on the station, so I had to get it by telephone. They were not at all hopeful. Gale warnings were out for the night and the next day bad weather was forecast with low cloud, rain and strong south-westerly winds.

The next day proved the forecast accurate. I rang up again to find my destination airfield, Worthy Down, had a cloud base of 50-100ft. As I could not see over the Cotswolds from where I was, there was absolutely no possibility of taking off. Other airfields en route were giving equally bad reports. As our instructions for 'Priority One' aircraft were to remain with the machine at all times and take it at the first moment the weather made it possible, I spent the whole day at Flying Control, or on the tarmac ringing up the Met people every half hour.

Eventually I had a quick lunch and on my return again phoned the Met. They told me that Worthy Down was now giving 500-600ft cloud base and there was an improvement of visibility at several places en route. Out of the window eastwards there was one point where there was a slight gap over the Costwold hills. In my anxiety to get airborne again, and being only in contact with the Met Office by telephone, I made a stupid and inexcusable mistake. I completely forgot to ask the strength of the wind, either at Worthy Down or generally. Had I done this I would never have taken off. As it was I announced my intention to try and get through. The CO of the airfield looked doubtful and told me that the wind was very strong. This I knew, but said I thought it might be better the other side of the Cotswolds. He detailed two men to each wing-tip to aid me taxiing out and, having checked everything, I opened up to full throttle and took off.

The plane was airborne in the shortest time I can ever remember and the moment it was off the ground I knew I had made a terrible mistake. The turbulence was terrific and the aircraft pitched and was buffeted about in a way that I have not experienced before or since. I throttled back slightly and clutched the stick in both hands in an attempt to keep the aircraft in a half-way normal position. I kept straight ahead, but was convinced I could not handle the aircraft under these conditions. The question was 'what to do?' I did'nt think I could turn back and land without crashing. I thought I would undoubtedly crash anyway, but at least it would be better to do it en route or at the airfield of my destination.

I steered for my gap in the Cotswolds. expecting the wings or tailplane to break off at any moment. The Swordfish however, was a soundly constructed machine and able to take fairly great stresses. It certainly had to do so on this occasion! Fortunately my harness was tightly adjusted, for my weight was hardly ever on the seat! No bucking horse I have ever ridden flung me about as wildly as this aircraft did.

Over the Cotswolds the turbulence was even worse; the aircraft was at the mercy of tremendously strong up and downdraughts, which fortunately were more 'up' than 'down'. On the other side of the Cotswolds the turbulence was less, but I realised by my drift that the wind was gale force. I was moving like a crab in relation to the ground, and rather slowly at that. The visibility had greatly improved however, and the green expanse of Worthy Down could be seen long before arrival. I remember thinking, with great relief, that it was a grass airfield and not runways, so landing dead into wind might be alright. I tried to do a circuit, but it was one which would not have passed the most elementary flying test. The wind-socks were standing horizontally; accordingly, I made an approach with plenty of throttle until close to the ground. When I throttled back, the ground-crew said afterwards that the machine flew backwards in relation to the ground! I was not aware of this myself, but as I landed the aircraft it did not roll forward more than a yard and I had to keep over half throttle to hold her in this position. I did not dare attempt to move or taxi. My only thought was one of huge relief. 'I've got here and it's still in one piece' The crash tender came out and about six ground-crew attached themselves to both my wings and tail so that with their assistance we taxied the machine over to the tarmac where I switched off and left them to battle with the job of putting it into a hangar.

I reported to Flying Control and was later told that the Captain wanted to see me. The Fleet Air Arm stations ashore were highly naval; they were all HMS something, and the Captain was the CO. He was rather terse. Apparently a grave breach of Naval discipline had been committed by my landing on a day when all their flying had been cancelled.

On reporting back to my Ferry Pool at Hamble the CO there promptly sent for me. The Navy had launched an official complaint that girls should not be allowed to fly aircraft about in weather that was considered completely unsuitable by their most experienced pilots. She asked me for an explanation. 'It was a Priority One Swordfish'. Margot found this hard to believe until she checked with Operations. With Priority One aircraft we were instructed to fly to the limit of our ability and the Swordfish had been delivered to the right place undamaged. As always, she backed me up. 'If it was a Priority One it was perfectly justified. You were quite in order'.

I ommitted to tell her that for the most part of the flight I had decided it was way beyond the limit of my ability! On this, as on other occasions, I was lucky.

June:
"I had a red chit 'Priority One' for Benson airfield; only for a Proctor, but fully tanked up, and on taxi-ing to the Control Tower, being told to leave the engine running and give my place to an RAF pilot and two very inconspicuous girls, dressed in drab civvies who were then being immediately dropped in France as agents. In less than an hour they would be in enemy territory. It was a sobering thought".

Betty Keith-Jopp alongside a Spitfire

Hamble only had Class II pilots and above. Their main job was to clear the factories in this rather vulnerable area: Supermarines at Eastleigh producing Spitfires; Cunliffe Owen, also there; Air Service Training at Hamble itself, repairing Spitfires; Vickers satellites; Airspeeds at Christchurch and Portsmouth. Many of these could be reached by car and so there was not the same need for Class I taxi pilots, and not many Class I aircraft, but a large variety of fighter aircraft. In 1944 and '45 these were mostly Spitfires, Hurricanes, Mustangs, Tempests, Typhoons, Fireflies as well as the FAA Walrus and Sea Otter, used for Air-Sea Rescue, and twin engined Oxfords from Christchurch. The CO Margot Gore, was liked and respected by all, She flew four-engined aircraft too, along with Rosemary Rees and Phillipa Bennett.

Jeffrey Quill, in his book 'Spitfire' says *before long every Spitfire which left our works was collected by a woman. In their dark blue uniforms they always looked neat and smart, and they did the job quietly and efficiently with the minimum of fuss'.*

CHAPTER SEVEN
Escapes and Incidents

Betty Keith-Jopp

One of the most amazing incidents of the war occurred to Betty Keith Jopp, when she survived a descent to the bottom of the Firth of Forth in a Fairey Barracuda. Betty, fair-haired. modest and unassuming, had been a former MT driver in the WAAF and then re-mustered as a radio operator.

'I remember sitting in a railway train at the beginning of the war and reading in a newspaper that the ATA had just been formed. ATA seemed an impossible dream to me".

However, when the opportunity came, she put her name forward along with all the others, and was put on the Air Ministry short list for an interview.

She puts her ultimate acceptance down to the fact that her uncle was one of the first to join the ATA; he was a legend himself, having been a fighter pilot in the first World War, and having lost one arm and an eye. In spite of this he remained in ATA from beginning to end and delivered well over 1,000 operational aircraft.

At the end of May 1945, Barbara Lankshear and Betty took off from Prestwick with Barracudas to Lossiemouth, but ran into bad weather. When crossing the Firth of Forth the cloud got lower and lower until it and the sea met. Barbara climbed up through the cloud ' a most unpleasant introduction to blind flying' and eventually landed at Donibristle, but Betty tried to turn back, and in doing so, hit the water. The Barracuda sank like a brick and almost before she realised what had happened, she was on the sea-bed with water squirting in at her from all directions. Betty hastily undid her safety harness and had her hand on the hood ejection lever when she realised she still had her parachute on and had to release that too,. As the Barracuda had air in the Observers Cabin below, which was forced up by the water pressure into the cockpit, when she jettisoned the hood the resultant bubble of air shot her up to the surface with some force.

She was not a strong swimmer and it was practically impossible to see in which direction to swim anyway because of the fog.

"It was very cold in the sea but fortunately I was only in overalls and shoes, not flying boots, so I could swim for a bit".

Skipper David Morris of the St Monance motor fishing boat '*Provide*' was late returning to port owing to having had engine trouble - he noticed something in the water and altered course. It was not a seal as he first thought, but a pilot! He picked her up, warming her with the contents of their Thermos flask and they were flabbergasted to find her a 'her' when taking off her flying helmet revealed her lovely fair hair!.

They took her to Anstruther harbour, where Betty remembers being

A poor quality , but nevertheless important photograph that shows Betty Keith-Jopp alongside a Barracuda similar to the one she was forced to ditch in the Firth of Forth.

hauled up on a stretcher and being put to bed in the Crail Fleet Air Arm hospital under a heated cradle. She returned to Prestwick the next day, apparently not much the worse for her extraordinary experience. She did fly a bit more after this, but the war in Europe was over and ATA had started to close its Pools.

"I cannot say that I enjoyed it any more, having moved from the stage 'it cannot happen to me' to 'it probably will!'".

She left ATA in August and subsequently got married. Betty now lives in South Africa and has two daughters.

Most pilots make mistakes, and we were no exception. A very senior ATA pilot, who shall remain nameless, after picking up five others in the Anson set his compass 180 degrees out by putting North on South. It was hazy and it was some time before the others aboard plucked up the courage to tell him!

Peggy did the same on her own once, in bad visibility, and it was more luck than judgement that stopped her flying into the Cardington Balloon barrage. If one was lucky, one learnt by one's mistakes and didn't make the same one again. If unlucky, they could prove fatal. The ATA lost well over 100 pilots during the war, fourteen of whom were women. Many of these accidents were due to mechanical failure or other circumstances beyond the pilots control, but others were due to pilot error or bad judgement. The seventeen WAAF ab initio pilots all survived, luck and good training being on their side.

Quite a few girls who had previous flying experience but had originally been turned down by ATA as having too little flying experience (200 hours was the minimum to start with) had joined the WAAF. As the war progressed, the number of ferry pilots needed increased, and the required flying hours decreased. Several re-applied to the ATA and were accepted.

One of these was Dolores Theresa Sorour, from

South Africa, who was stationed at Hamble and was always known as Jackie. She had learnt to fly at 16 and was accepted by the ATA in July 1940 - and stayed on to the very end. She was one of the youngest pilots, but in a couple of years had built up an amazing amount of experience and technical knowledge. She was dark haired, attractive and slim and at 24, still looked 17. She was qualified on all singles and twin engined aircraft and suffered for many years under the all-to-frequent male assumption that an attractive young female was not able to be trusted with an aircraft. She was a good actress and had her own way of dealing with this. Once, when she was delivering Spitfire XIVs with two other girl pilots, one of the latter had her Air Speed Indicator stick at 240 mph, a very unpleasant thing to happen, as it is then very difficult to judge your approach speed. So she made a long, precautionary approach before a successful landing. Later, when they were lunching together in the Mess, an RAF Officer at the same table rather sarcastically asked Jackie '...was it you making an approach from London with flaps down all the way?' 'Flaps?' replied Jackie, looking at him innocently 'I did not know they had flaps' Stickly silence. Playing along with her, the girl concerned said 'Its that funny shaped lever on the dashboard' 'Oh' said Jackie ' I wondered what it was for!' Horrified masculine faces all round. Finally, a more senior officer at the end of the table said 'I think they are having us on, chaps'.

She later proved her initiative and determination by hitch-hiking to South Africa and back by air to see her sick mother. She got there and back in a week, via Malta, Cairo, going, and via Khartoum and Istres returning!

Dora Lang was another pilot at Hamble who had come in from the WAAF with previous flying experience. Fair-haired, tall and reserved, she was, unfortunately one of the few women pilots killed when a Mosquito she was ferrying crashed on landing at Lasham on 2 March 1944.

Light aircraft were sometimes easier to fly in bad weather as their ground-speed was low and it was easier to see where one was going. Still, they posed other problems. The Tiger Moth had a stalling speed, with one pilot in it of about 40 miles an hour, so that if the wind was gusting up to gale force it would get airborne on its own unless firmly tied down, or if in the air would remain airborne!.

Ruth remembers taking a Tiger Moth to a Training School on top of a Down (possibly Cliffe Pypard) and trying to get it to land: "On my third attempt they had enough men out to hold the wing-tips and pull me down the last six inches". On another occasion she landed in sea fog at what turned out to be an American Flying Fortress base in East Anglia: "Once on the ground I only had about 20 metres visibility and taxied until I found grass and stayed there until I was found. The indignity of parking my plane under the wing of a Fortress!. Because the base was fully operational and there were no women, I was locked away for three days, only an officer came to take me for meals!"

Barbara remembers the narrow runways of the Fleet Air Arm airfields, considered adequate for training pilots who were to land on carriers. Also how, if the aircraft had folding wings sailors would swarm all over the machine and had the wings folded before one was hardly down from the aircraft!

Rosemary, who had been flying a Fairchild with very bad brakes on taxi work tipped it onto its nose next time as they had meanwhile put on new brakes.

The Maintenance Units to which they ferried to and from did their work in hangars, but their offices were often insignificant little huts at the side where we had to go for our necessary paperwork. Nevertheless, the ground crews were often most welcoming; none who had to go into Wroughton are likely to forget Ted who was in charge there and knew them all and always produced a welcome cup of tea. Ferry pilots and ground engineers were all just one small part of a chain to provide the RAF and FAA with aircraft.

Winifred 'Pooh' Stokes

Known to all as 'Pooh' from the A A Milne 'Winnie the Pooh', she was one of the first intake:
"I was at Sherburn with several pilots waiting for the weather to improve before take-off. At around 1pm we were told we could go. Not a very good decision as most of us had to make a forced landing. I landed my Swordfish in a field at Northampton. I spent the night at a house on the edge of the field. A big gathering there by the time I got out of the aircraft! In the morning we put on quite a good show. A Fairchild landed bringing a spare pilot who flew the Swordfish out and I was flown out in the Fairchild"

Before that she and Diana Faunthorpe flew Swordfish over to Northern Ireland. Pooh and Di had become friends at Haddenham and did most of their training and postings together. They became known to the rest of us as 'the inseparables'. Both tall, with an air of competence and authority, Pooh had a caustic wit and Di was the perfect foil for her, quiet and reserved, never minding the arrows that sometimes flew. They took the Swordfish from High Ercall to Cark on the rugged north-west coast, where they had to put down on account of bad weather. They spent the night in the sick-bay as there was no other accommodation available! The next day they flew to Kirkbride, once again stopping the night before taking off the next morning across the sea to Maydown. 'It was all very exciting. The first time we had flown over the sea'. They were picked up from there by an Anson from the Belfast Pool; the next day they flew back to England in a Stirling which was being ferried to Hullavington. They both returned to Thame for Class II training in the New Year and, after completing the ground course, started flying the Harvard in February and soloed the Spitfire within a day of each other three weeks later.

CHAPTER EIGHT
Class II training and ferrying

After a winter of Class I ferrying, the instructions that came to report for Class II Instruction back at Thame were received with great excitement. What so many of the female pilots had thought would never be possible now appeared to be within reach of all. After the usual spell of ground school, flying instruction started in the Harvard. The Allies were now rapidly advancing into Germany; it really seemed as though the end of the war was in sight, and everyone was keen to get qualified on Class II before this happened. The Harvards, those noisy, powerful aircraft, were the first ones the girls had

Class II groundschool at Thame in March 1945. (L to R) Henry and Aimée watch Henry and Katie supposedly at work!

met with retractable undercarriages and were interesting and not too difficult to fly.

Rosemary came down after one flight and told Barbara: "My instructor said to me 'I told you to level off about the height of a double decker bus, not the bloody Eiffel Tower' After a few hours dual however, everyone soloed on the Harvard without any trouble. The next thing of course, was the Spitfire. As they had all been used to flying strange types solo, the idea of being on ones

In full uniform Frankie, Aimee and Ruth inspect a Harvard at White Waltham

own did not worry anyone, and after the Harvard, it did not seem too difficult. For many this was the high spot of their flying career; at last they felt that they could do the job as well as their male counterparts. On the whole they hard a fairly tough time in the male-dominated Air Force world and had to try hard to avoid being helpless females at all times. They wanted first and foremost to be treated as professionals who could step into what had been previously considered a man's job - and do it with maximum efficiency. They had the marvellous example of women pilots who had been in the ATA much longer than them and were determined to follow in their footsteps, or perhaps one should say slipstream!.

Katie:
"I had one scary experience, all of my own making. I'd solo'd the Spitfire for the first time in the morning. An all-time 'high', the height of my ambitions. The only Spitfires used by the school heated up very fast on the ground and

we had been warned that if you started a take-off above a certain temperature, the engine would seize up. It was a warm day, and other people had used the plane of course. When I got out to it in the afternoon for my turn it was still very hot, and I had to wait half an hour for it to cool off. After a 'high' an anti-climax often sets in; waiting for the engine to cool, my confidence cooled also. I got airborne, then lost my nerve completely about landing. I'd get within ten feet of the ground and just could not get down that last bit. I'd open up and go round again. On one circuit I saw Flight-Captain Marks riding his bike out to the Control Car. I finally got down and wanted nothing more than to stay down, but Marks waved his arms frantically and I had to go off again. I finally landed three times. When reporting the number at the school, Flight-Captain Marks said '...correction, ONE landing, two arrivals!'"

After the successful Spitfire flight, they were finished with Class II training and were promoted to First Officers. This meant an increase in pay and the right to put on a broad gold band on the shoulders of their uniforms.

The Mustang and other American aircraft demonstrated the importance of the ATA 5' 5" height requirement. Peggy got her first Mustang at Hamble and, unlike the Spitfire, whose rudder could be adjusted for the shortest of legs and everything was close to hand, the Mustang was much larger and nothing adjusted sufficiently.

"It had toe brakes and on testing these out when I first climbed into the cockpit, I found I could not operate them. By tucking my overnight bag behind my back so that I was a bit further forward, I discovered that I could just manage it., although in doing so I could only just keep my eyes above the level of the cockpit and my face was unpleasantly close to the gun-sight. In most single-seat fighters this was pretty close to your face anyway and I had already seen the results in hospital to faces thrown forward on to them, so it was not a pleasant feeling.

In the air however, it was a lovely machine to fly; it would trim perfectly and flew fast and steadily 'hands off'. On my first landing I put, or tried to put, the undercarriage lever down. I found I could only push the lever to the 'down' position with the very tips of my fingers. On final approach my undercarriage suddenly retracted on me and I had to go around again. I realised that I could not get it into the fully ,locked-down position and in order to do this I was obliged to undo my safety harness and landed with it undone. I always had this trouble with Mustangs, though in future I did my straps up very loosely so I could get the necessary reach forward and still have something to hold me a bit in case of emergency".

Taxi-ing on narrow perimeter tracks was also a problem on this and other long-nosed fighters if the pilot was a bit on the short side, but by continual zig-zagging, one could look out each side alternately. In those days there were still very few nosewheel aircraft.

Ruth Russell was another who found the Mustang and other American aircraft difficult. After her unfortunate experience whilst training at Barton, when she returned there for training in June 'Captain Wood took very special precautions before he let me go solo...   ...I think he expected me to loose my nerve'. Not Ruth. In August she finished on Proctors at Thame, did Cross Country Flight in September and was posted to the Training Pool in November. She did a months secondment at Prestwick, followed by '...a boring month of Fairchild taxi work at No. 6 Ferry Pool at Ratcliffe and then back to Class I ferrying at Thame'. Towards the end of March she started Class II training on Harvards.

"My first Spitfire was a Mk. Vb on 19 April 1945, a year and a day after my accident.

May 1st found me at No. 7 Ferry Pool at Sherburn in Elmet. Here I added Barracudas and a Spitfire Mk. IX in the first few weeks, then amongst new ones were Reliant, Martinet, Hellcat, Hurricane II and IV, Mustangs and a Firefly. Later I added Barracuda varieties (with nobs on),

Wildcat, Seafire, Corsairs and a Sea Otter (which came complete with boat-hook and anchor!).

I found the American planes difficult as they were designed for six foot tall men with long legs. Cushions brought my face too near the gun-sight as several of the others found. I left ATA at the break up at the end of September.

I had a few frights - such as a burst tyre on landing in a Hellcat when I thought I was going over, but didn't. I remember going to 10,000ft over the Welsh border in a Spitfire to do an illegal roll. I had done quite a bit of aerobatics in Tigers (dual) and got myself briefed by the RAF: I just had to do it once - it was fine!"

Summer 1944 Left to Right: Betty Keith-Jopp, Sue Alexander, Jean Arthur (Henry) Ruth Russell, Annette Mahon, Aimee de Neve and Katie Smith

All who flew the Spitfire will always remember it, from the little puffs of smoke when the Merlin engine started, to the 'popping' of the exhaust as you throttled back coming into land. It was a lovely aircraft to fly and fitted the smallest of them.

June:
"The day I first went solo in a Spitfire was tremendous. Through friends connected with the Free French I came up to a Grosvenor House Ball that night to help entertain a bunch of the Maquis lads who had been over for debriefing and instructions, and were due to return to France the following day. I had been asked to help host the party as my French was pretty fluent. Being the only female in uniform, and being on an absolute 'high' from having flown my first Spitfire, and wearing a much-coverted and glamorous uniform, it was a pretty terrific night!

I always equated the Spitfire to a pure thoroughbred; the finesse and spirit was so similar in both, nothing could come up to that wonderful feeling of having a superb mount under one".

Annette Mahon

"On Class II I was always OK with landings, but my take-offs left a lot to be desired, so during my first Spitfire solos I was determined to get it right.

The first two take-offs weren't too bad, but not good enough so on my third I flew straight as an arrow, selecting undercarriage up and going through the gate with ease. Feeling pleased with myself I settled down to

Dr S.M.B. Hill, Medical Officer at Thame and Annette Mahon. They were married in 1947.

99

enjoy the joys of the Spitfire. The temperature was quite high and I remembered our instructions to fly around for a while to let the temperature drop. I did this for twenty minutes or so, but the temperature was getting higher and higher. I was in a literal sweat as the petrol gauge was showing low. What to do? Nothing for it but to land. Down wind, cross wind and then crab in for the last 45 degrees. Then I saw them. The blood wagon, fire engine and all. I looked around to see who was in trouble, as they only came out for an emergency. Could not see anything amiss and I landed with the biggest bump you could imagine. At the end of the landing strip I switched off as the temperature was terrific. My instructor drove up to me and asked what I was up to in not-so-polite terms. I explained, and he said I had been flying around with one undercarriage leg down over the air intake and on the ground everyone thought it was a malfunction and that I could not get both wheels down - hence the panic. My boyfriend, the doctor who was in the ambulance turned to the driver and said 'They've locked down all right after that dreadful landing!' It took quite a while to live that one down".

Not all made it however. Frankie:
"On the day I was to take up a Spitfire I was sitting outside in the sunshine with others waiting my turn. The Adj came out with our letters which had just arrived. Goody! ... One from Canada - home! In it my mother told me that my father was going into hospital for a major operation and he enclosed a 'goodbye' letter to me, just in case.

I adored my father ...had his adventurous spirit, which had brought me to England, the WAAF and hence the ATA. I rushed into the Adj's office and told him I would have to go home immediately.

I never flew the Spitfire. Was taken immediately to White Waltham... resigned from ATA and hoped to fly home as soon as possible. My father recovered, thank goodness and I have never been sorry that I took the action I did on that fateful day as my Dad meant more to me that any Spitfire. Anyway, I was qualified to fly it, like others who did on that day - 25 April 1945.

I stayed with my parents in Canada until July 1946 when I joined my husband Fergus in Jamaica. In 1948 we went to British Guiana where my son was born in 1949".

Aimée de Neve

Aimée de Neve was one of the second group to come to ATA for Ab Initio training. She was another war-widow who had been married to a pilot, a Squadron leader in the Netherlands Air Force. Her impressions of Class II training:

"Very exciting! The Harvard felt so powerful after all the light aircraft and Marks (her instructor) liked to give me quite frightening shocks to make sure I was awake! My first Spitfire flight was unbelievable! This beautiful

"My first Spitfire was unbelievable..." Aimée de Neve at Ratcliffe

aircraft was actually all mine for a brief time. I was rather worried when I had to do several circuits, as an RAF aircraft had done a belly landing and I had all the red flares etc thrown at me"

DH89 Dominie of the RAF serialledR9565 with two ATA girls alongside. The type was used by the ATA for its original purpose - as an airliner to ferry pilots around.

CHAPTER NINE
End of the war in Europe

Peggy:
"At the beginning of May I had a few days leave. It was while I was home with my mother that we heard the announcement that Germany had capitulated and that the war in Europe was over. I instantly got on a train and went up to London. Months before, a group of us had agreed that wherever we found ourselves we would do everything possible to meet up that evening at the Brevet Flying Club which was then in Charles Street just off Berkley Square.

When I arrived there I could not get inside the door. This club, whose membership was limited to those with pilot's or observer's brevets on their uniforms, had been a favourite meeting place for some years. One had always been able to get first class meals there despite the rationing. Tonight it was filled to overflowing with pilots of every nationality. The window to the street was open and tankards of beer were passed out to us through the open window. It was 'on the house' that night.

The all-womens Ferry Pilot's Pool at Hamble.

There was a great deal of noisy shouting, singing and dancing in the streets. Later, we all went to Buckingham Palace where an enormous throng of people had gathered who were yelling for the Royal family. They came out several times onto the balcony and waved to the cheering crowds who remained there until well after midnight. A lot of people had came to London to celebrate the peace and most of them had made no arrangements for staying the night. Fortunately it was a balmy night, because I think large numbers had to be content with benches in the park! About 2 am it dawned on us that we too ought to find somewhere to sleep. I rang several friends but got no reply, they were all out celebrating too! I went to the Overseas League where I was a member and I knew there was a night porter, but he told me that there was no chance of a bed - they had all been taken a long time ago. He said that as it was a rather special night, however, he would make an exception and allow me to sleep on a couch in the writing room. This was most comfortable and he even brought me a cup of tea in the morning to make sure I vacated my emergency sleeping place before it was required for its usual purposes!

We wondered what was going to happen to ATA. We were told that although fighting had ceased in Europe, the war was not over, for we were still fighting Japan. Ferrying would go on as before for some time, but on a gradually diminishing scale. There would be a lot of old aircraft to be flown to aircraft parks for breaking up - however, those pilots who wished to leave were free to do so. Some of the American pilots returned to their own country and some volunteered to leave. Most of the WAAF were determined to stay on as long as they would have us.

We collected a lot of Spitfires from various fighter stations; battle-scarred, decorated and sometimes with papers marked 'Not entirely airworthy - serviceable for one flight only'. We took these rather gingerly, but often they were beautiful aircraft. One in particular had 14 crosses on it and undoubtedly belonged to some well-known and decorated fighter pilot. It seemed very sad to land it for the last time and park it in a row of other Spits already getting rusty waiting for disposal or breaking up".

They heard that the Womens' Pool at Hamble would be closed down. There was a farewell party and many of the pilots returned to civilian life after this. A few who had not elected to go were posted to other pools. Sheila decided to leave and returned to America and Peggy was posted, with Veronica Volkers to Whitchurch, Bristol.

Aimée was posted to the Ratcliffe Pool. This airfield belonged to Sir Lindsey Everard and had been a private flying club before the war. It was a mixed pool, with some very experienced pilots.

June:
"I was billeted at Ratcliffe Hall with Sir Lindsey and Lady Everard. They had 12 pilots staying with them and we had the privilege of meeting Winston Churchill and Handley Page at dinner several times"

Ratcliffe was not an easy pool to ferry from, being in a very hazy area and one often surrounded by industrial fog. It had one advantage however, in that it was right beside the old roman Fosse Way, a wonderful landmark and one followed gratefully by many ATA pilots on their way to and from the airfields and MUs to the north and south. If the visibility got too bad they could always drop in at, or turn back to, Ratcliffe.

Aimee ferried six different types of Class II aircraft whilst she was there and left when all the rest did at the end of September. She married again in 1945 and had three children, two sons and a daughter. She found time though to do some interesting post war flying, of which more later.

Sue and Katie were also at No. 5 Ferry Pool at Ratcliffe that last summer of 1945 before the Japanese surrender. They had done an R/T course after their Class II, it having been decided, but rather too late, that it would be useful for pilots to have some air-to-ground communication at last. Although most of the aircraft flown from the factories did not have any R/T fitted, those from the MUs to the squadrons did, also those being taken back for modification or repair. With the end of the war in Europe, the necessity for keeping radio silence, in order not to give any information to the enemy had ceased.

Katie:
"My biggest adventure came in July 1945. I was stationed at Ratcliffe and it was my turn to fly the taxi Fairchild. I took off with three passengers for a factory airfield just east of Birmingham. I delivered them and took off again so as to meet them at their destination. At approximately 300 feet the engine failed. Our training when that happened on take-off was to land straight ahead... but, straight ahead there was nothing but the roof-tops of Birmingham! I did a 180 degree turn back to the airfield. The engine kicked in for a few moments, which helped, then quit for good. I missed the hangar roof by inches, and then did a heavy landing on the grass, breaking the undercarriage and tipping on my nose. Firm ground never felt so good, and I still have the tip of that prop!

Later I found that the service crew at Ratcliffe had run and run that engine, expecting it to quit. When it did'nt, they let it go. The pay-off was that later that same day HQ phoned Ratcliffe and asked them to send in Fairchild 477, it was due to be broken up. Our Operations cheerfully told them not to worry, we'd already broken it up for them!"

Katie married her US friend the previous month and was now Mrs Hirsch. She was released from ATA with the majority of us in September 1945 and returned to the United States with her husband, where she raised a family. Both she and her husband became involved with theatrical work, thus reviving their original interests and are still active in this pursuit.

Annette:
"I had quite a few scares during my ferrying days. An ex-RAF pilot and myself each had a Martinet to deliver from Hawarden to Kirkbride. The cloud base was between 600 and 800 feet at Hawarden, but the Met Office forecast clear at Kirkbride. The RAF pilot, with experience of instrument flying said he would take off and if I took off immediately after him all would be OK as he would lead the way. Unfortunately I had never flown a Martinet before and this one had a drogue arm, so I was not prepared for the extent of swing on take-off. It was a vicious swing, missing the Control Tower on the left by inches and then up through the clouds into the beautiful blue sky. I looked round and round, but the other Martinet was nowhere to be seen. I did not know where I was, because all I could see was an impenetrable blanket of fluffy white clouds below.

I was really frightened and decided to head north and hope for the best. I flew on for 40 minutes or so, each moment seeming like an hour, regretting ever having taken such a stupid decision to follow an aircraft. Miraculously the clouds dispersed and I managed to locate myself on the map. What a relief! I landed at Kirkbride and the RAF pilot greeted me with 'It was easy was'nt it?'

I wish I could convey the sense of panic I had flying above the clouds without a radio, and as I look back I realise how foolhardy I was. Were we all a bit foolhardy, or was it just me?

Another time I was ferrying a Barracuda from Prestwick to Hawarden and as I was passing over the hills of Dumfriesshire, I thought I could smell the Heather in full bloom below me. Enjoying the experience, I continued on for quite a time. Suddenly I looked down into the cockpit and there I saw a broken pipe with fluid coming out all over my flying boots. This was the smell! I tried to think calmly what it could be and was it dangerous. I decided to seek out the nearest aerodrome which was Wigtown. All was quiet there and, hoping that my flaps, undercarriage and brakes would work if the fluid was hydraulic, I landed safely but found I had no control of the brakes. I managed to slow up only a bit when the Barracuda swung viciously into the intersection and later I managed to stop. I went to the Control Tower and a young pilot there said 'That was quite a nifty bit of taxi-ing the way you swung into the intersection'. Needless to say, I didn't disillusion him!"

148 RAF pilots who had been released to ATA were recalled; they had had ferry training and could now undertake the same job in the RAF. At the beginning of June, MAP sent a letter to ATA saying that after the middle of the month ATA should be responsible only for the ferrying of aircraft from Constructors and Repair Units to Maintenance Units; ferrying to service users would be done by service pilots. Between 30 June and 31 December ATA should take steps to reduce their personnel and pools. After 31 December ferrying would be done by RAF pilots of 41 Group.

ATA accordingly closed most of the pools successively. No. 1 Pool at White Watham would be the last to close, but other pilots would be given three months pay in lieu of notice and would finish on 29 September. This was sad news for the WAAF, who had nearly all passed their Class II and would now only have a rather limited amount of ferrying on these types, although the Fleet Air Arm still had quite a lot of work for the ATA for a few months.

The war in the Far East was still going on and as they had not such a large reserve of pilots as the RAF, most of the ATA managed to get a chance to deliver from four to eight different Class II types and some pools were still quite busy, owing to the closure of others. Still, towards the end there was less and less work and everyone had more time off than before.

Sue and Katie, posted to Ratcliffe, used to go hay-making as there were quite a few days without jobs. Sue had a horse at a nearby farm. Pooh and Di were at White Waltham, so were flying up to the end. They, together with June and Henry, had a very varied lot of types; Henry flew a Tempest. At the end of June, Henry, June and Pooh went over the Channel to Courtrai in an Anson to bring back some Army Austers. Unfortunately they were all unserviceable except one, which June flew back; the others had to return in the Anson. It was an interesting trip abroad however, and a chance to see a bit of battle-scarred France. Peggy, who had been posted to Whitchurch near Bristol when Hamble closed had already completed her Class III course at White Waltham in April and could now fly twin engined aircraft, including the taxi Anson.

The ferry pool at Whitchurch, to which Peggy had been posted with Veronica Volkers, had up to this point been staffed entirely by men. The CO had refused to have any women posted there. He accepted them with some reluctance and Peggy and Veronica felt very much like new girls at school when they first went there. They were both keen Bridge players and found several others who were, too, and they soon became half-way accepted.

ATA were now ferrying the first jet aircraft from Moreton Vallance where the Gloster Aircraft Company was producing and test-flying Meteors. All the pilots wanted to fly one and those at Bristol and Aston Down had the best chance, being the nearest pools. Veronica Volkers was the first woman to fly one, she had been in ATA since 1941 and was a Flight Captain. Peggy had too little twin engined experience, so never got her hands on one, but had to be content with flying Oxfords and Ansons.

She had to fetch an Oxford from Christchurch one

day and noticed that it was very old and had been recently repaired after a crash:

"I was flying at about 3000 feet when suddenly there was a most frightful noise and the whole aircraft vibrated like mad. 'This is it' I thought, but automatically closed both throttles and put the machine into a glide. The vibration was less, but still intense, and I gently opened the throttles in turn and found that the Port engine seemed to want to jump out of its casing. I switched it off at once and trimmed to single engined flight and found the Starboard engine was quite normal and the vibration had ceased. I had lost quite a bit of height and now had to decide how far I could go on one engine. It would not climb at all on one engine - and would only just hold its height. I decided to land at the nearest airfield, which was a Fleet Air Arm station, Yeovilton, just ahead of me. Of course there was no R/T in the aircraft, so I could not contact Control who gave me a flashing red light - the signal to go and land elsewhere.

The runway was clear as I approached, so I waggled my wings as a distress signal, put down my undercarriage and flaps and noticed there was no landing T at the end of the runway, but also that there was no wind. I then saw to my horror that a number of small naval aircraft were approaching me from the opposite direction! A series of red Very lights were fired from Control and about four naval aircraft broke off and climbed away in different directions. I landed and rolled to a stop towards the end of the runway. The only way to turn off it was to the right. With my left engine out I found this impossible; the brakes and rudder were not sufficient to offset its tendency to turn left. After having gone around in a circle I stayed where I was.

A car from Control arrived and an irate naval officer got out. 'What do you mean by landing here against a red? Not only do you do that, but you hold up all landings by remaining at the end of the runway. That is what happens when they let women fly aircraft!' His last remark annoyed me somewhat. 'You try turning to the right with only a right engine and see if you can do it'. He looked at my port engine. 'I'm sorry...' he said '...I didn't see it. I'll send for some help'. They soon had me towed in.

When I got out of the aircraft, I saw at once what the trouble was. A large chunk of propeller blade was missing! It had not been possible for me to see this from the cockpit due to the position it had stopped in. I had been lucky, as when this happens the resultant out-of-balance forces can be so great that the engine is torn completely out of its mounting, with much graver consequences. Back at Whitchurch the CO wanted to know what had happened. He thought it was due to low flying as there was no indication that I had hit a bird. I told him that I did not indulge in that pastime, but I had a feeling that he did not believe me. A later check however showed that the propeller had been repaired and it had broken in exactly the same place. Once again on the accident report I was not held responsible!"

It is all over...
In August 1945 the first Atom bomb was dropped on Japan, followed by another a few days later - on the 15th came news of Japan's surrender, the end of the war had finally come! Everyone was glad that all hostilities had finished, but several ATA girls felt that it was also the end of a life to which they were growing more and more attached.

Ferrying continued at a few pools until the middle to end of September; those who had no leave were given it and those of the WAAF who wanted to return to their WAAF trades could do so. The WAAF however, did not want them back, for they were dismissing thousands themselves. It would mean a lot of extra work to re-equip those from the ATA and then dismiss them - they could stay with the ATA until the end of the month when they would be given three months pay in lieu of notice - Most stayed.

On 29 September 1945 a final Air Display was held at White Waltham, open to the public. This was in aid of the ATA Benevolent Fund, which had been formed to help wives and children of those pilots that had been killed whilst engaged on ferrying duties. The weather was perfect and many aircraft manufacturers sent aircraft for both static and flying displays by their test pilots, which was terrific. It was a great success and a considerable sum was raised.

For many in ATA it was a final re-union. All went round looking at everything and having refreshments together. Future prospects were discussed, which did not seem too hopeful. The following day, those who had not handed in their flying and other equipment did so and received in return their official discharge, along with three months pay, which was a very nice gratuity.

By November, all the pools had been closed with the exception of White Waltham, which carried on with the winding up process until they too closed on 30 November. It was all over.

CHAPTER TEN
Post war

The prospects of a woman getting any kind of job during the winter of 1946/7 seemed pretty hopeless. Hundreds of well-trained, highly experienced RAF pilots were looking for jobs and only those with pre-war qualifications as commercial pilots or flying instructors, or with sufficient money to start their own businesses seemed to have a chance.

Three WAAF ATA girls had already found romance and had got married whilst in ATA. Frankie had been the first, getting married while still at Haddenham, to the boy she had met coming over from Canada on the boat.

Joyce Fenwick married another ATA pilot, Johnnie Tharp and left ATA in April 1945, owing to a rather unexpected pregnancy that was only discovered when she went to the sick bay complaining of nausea. Later she went to South Africa with her husband. Katie Stanley Smith married an American and went to the USA.

Annette Mahon, the lovely warm and dizzy Irish girl captured the heart of the station Medical officer, Dr Hill and married him two years after the war. It is interesting to

AIR TRANSPORT AUXILIARY
White Waltham Airfield,
Berkshire.

Any woman who becomes pregnant is deemed unfit to carry out flying duties.

Any woman pilot or woman flight-engineer who becomes pregnant must, in honesty, report the fact immediately to the Commandant Women or the Chief Medical Officer.

Stencil No 2267.

Pauline Gower Commander,
Commandant Women.

The standing order from Pauline Gower stating what to do if a pilot or Flight Engineer became pregnant!

note that he went back to sea as a ship's surgeon with City Line, and there was an apprentice on board that had rescued Betty Keith-Jopp when she was swimming about in the Firth of Forth after going down in the Barracuda. They had not seen the plane go down, only heard it!

Annette and her husband did some flying at the West London Flying Club afterwards, where Maurice passed his pilots' Licence with Bill Hampton and Joan Hughes as instructors, both of whom were ex-ATA.

She became Information Officer of the management team organising the International Air Tattoo, first at RAF Station Greenham Common and then at RAF Fairford. 'I enjoyed every moment of my involvement. It kept me in touch with the RAF and with great regret I retired after 12 years because of moving down to the New Forest'. She had three children and still lives in that part of the country.

Others followed their example soon after, or went their own way, going back to pre-war occupations or spending their gratuities on leave with their families, or riding, hunting, ski-ing or doing whatever the mood or fate invited. Few could afford to pay for flying, although a few small flying clubs had started operating.

Peggy started a riding school and hunting stable near Aylesbury:

"Several times I rode past the airfield at Haddenham, which was now hardly recognisable with all the weeds growing around the huts and hangars, and all the old memories would start flooding back. One clear spring day, when the sky was blue, i could bear it no longer and drove over to Luton where I knew there was a Flying Club. Enrolling as a member, I was told I must have a dual check on the Tiger Moth before being allowed to take it solo. After three circuits and landings the instructor was satisfied and, once again, the feeling of being free and away from the earth gave me the same deep pleasure and satisfaction".

They had a Proctor at Luton and this Peggy decided to hire and fly over to Ireland where her mother was staying at the time. Armed with nothing more than a passport and an overnight bag, which was all she thought was necessary, she landed at Liverpool to clear Customs, only to be disillusioned by a very dour Customs Officer, who told her she had none of the papers necessary for taking an aircraft abroad:

"Having got this far I was not going back and, by means of making a horrible nuisance of myself to everyone, managed to get a form out of someone and filled it out to Customs requirements. The Customs Officer was still very doubtful and did his best to put me off. Doubtless he thought that a woman was incapable of making such a flight! He told me that they probably would not let me land or take off again in Dublin; they might impound my aircraft; my form was only for English Customs. I was not perturbed. They obviously could not stop me landing in Dublin after a flight across the sea!

When I arrived at Dublin Airport, they could not have been more welcoming or hospitable. Ireland still had very few visitors in aircraft, and were extremely helpful. If there were any Customs, they certainly did not introduce themselves! I did not have to show any papers, or pay any landing fee; they found room for the aircraft in a hangar and arranged transport into town for me.

I spent a wonderful time there. Punchestown races were on. I did something I have never done before or since at a race meeting - I backed five out of the six winners which, even with the small bets that were on, represented sizable winnings! I went shopping in Dublin. The shops had a lot that was not available in austerity England and I stocked up with nylons and other goodies and still found that I had enough to pay all my expenses and the hire of the aircraft. Returning the Proctor to Luton, after a smooth entry through English Customs and an easy and informal departure from Ireland - where half of the airport staff seemed to turn out to wave me goodbye - I re-booked the Proctor for the International Air Rally at Deauville"

Peggy had arranged to fly to this with Mary and Monique, her house-mates at Hamble previously, and took the Proctor into Croydon to pick them up and clear Customs from there. It so happened that she had never landed there during the war and this was her first landing at Croydon as a pilot. She recalled how, in 1925 on her 8th birthday, she had had her first five minute joy-ride from there, never dreaming that one day she would be landing there as a pilot!

The annual rally at Deauville is famous. On this occasion it was very special - it was the first since war had ended. The town and the French coast were still looking very battle-scarred, with signs of damage everywhere. Most of Deauville needed repairing and painting, but it was surprising how quickly some of the better hotels had re-organised themselves so that once again there was an atmosphere of French luxury everywhere. The food was magnificent. One had forgotten, especially after years of rationing how good French food could be! There was a Gala dinner, with fireworks afterwards and one of the stars from the Paris opera sang the Marseillaise with so much feeling that many of the audience were in tears. Later, they all moved into the Casino, a first for the three women and all had beginners luck, so that they could drink Champagne and go shopping in the town the next day. They landed back at Croydon wondering what the Customs would say to all the French perfumes and cheeses - luckily they were very lenient as they realised what the temptations must have been after many years of being cut off from the continent.

Flying for pleasure like this, however, was a very expensive pastime. Suddenly they heard, in 1947, that women pilots were being accepted into the flying branch of the RAF Volunteer Reserve, providing they had the necessary qualifications. Immediately they had a lot of applications from ex-ATA women pilots, including

Rosemary Bonnet, Ruth Russell, Sue Alexander, Suzanne Chapman and Peggy Eveleigh.

As they were scattered round the countryside, they were not often at the same Reserve Centres, and often found themselves the only woman amongst the other male pilots. Each could only do 30 hours a year in their spare time at weekends, and a compulsory period of two weeks in uniform on the station. Once again, they were being paid to fly instead of having to pay for it! Better still, the RAF schedule had items on it which they had not been allowed to do in the ATA - night flying, instrument flying, aerobatics and formation flying. What is more, they had to do those things. The 30 hours per year could be extended to 60 if they could produce good grounds. This was easy as all the girls were below average in night flying and aerobatics.

Ruth Russell, after having done a little gliding, joined No.1 RAFVR at Panshangar:

"I found, without a car, it was difficult to get out there and gave up in mid-1948. I took a job a second-in-command in the Government Met Office at Bermuda in August of that year. I did three months or more at Prestwick International Airport as a refresher course and on trans-Atlantic work, forecasting upper level winds etc and went to Bermuda in late 1948. I met Keith (still my husband) there and we married quickly. He was stationed there with the British Army. I gave up forecasting a week before my son was born; a pity, as the job was very interesting indeed for shipping, local forecasts and hurricanes! For six months of this time I was in total command as the boss went away on long leave"

She now has four children and she and her husband run a cattle and sheep farm in Australia; her youngest daughter is an Air Hostess with QANTAS, the Australian airline.

Sue Alexander also joined the RAFVR (Flying) at No. 7 RFS at Desford, in 1947/8, was then abroad for a

Sue Alexander in full flying kit climbs aboard a DH82 Tiger Moth whilst serving with the RAFVR.

year and then resumed with No. 10 RFS at Exeter in 1950, where there were two other female pilots, Jackie Serour (now Moggridge) and a younger girl who had not been in the ATA:

"They got the three of us together to do some sort of all-female 'Fly Past' for an Air Display! By June 1952, I felt too out of touch to cope with lectures on aero-engines, gunnery etc which we had to do as well as the men did. I wrote a letter resigning on the grounds that I would not be of much use in the event of war and much too 'windy' to fly jets. That, would you believe was not grounds for release and I had to write another letter saying I could not find the time for training! Bureaucracy at its most ridiculous!'

She then concentrated on horses in Somerset and became quite well known as an Instructor. Rosemary Bonnet joined the RAFVR flying branch at Fairoaks. Here she met her future husband, who was also flying there. They both took out private pilots licences in 1948, but both only flew privately for a short time before getting married. Dick Towers, her husband had been flying with 670 Squadron in India, before, but he decided to give up flying and start farming in Wales where Rosemary could pursue her intense interest in horses. She bred, showed and hunted with a great deal of success, and they had one daughter.

Peggy, who had moved her stables down to Dorset, joined the nearest RAFVR branch which was, strangely enough, at Hamble, her former Ferry Pool.

"I was taken up for some dual formation flying for the first time, in Tiger Moths. When ferrying Spitfires we had sometimes formated on each other at a nice, respectable distance, but they were easy and steady aircraft compared with the Tiger Moth, which seemed to jump up and down all the time in relation to the other aircraft. On landing, my instructor asked me what I thought of it and I told him I had never been so terrified in my life. He roared with laughter and thought it was a huge joke, but it was absolutely true! With time and practice, I got slightly better at it, but always came to the conclusion that I could do without close companionship in the air!

We had to wear uniform during our two weeks continuous training, but at weekends we could fly in civilian clothes. This caused some surprise on occasions. We had a certain amount of hours to put in on cross-country flights and I was asked where I would like to go. I decided to visit my mother-in-law in Devon, so got permission to land at Chivenor, with a stop at the RAF Reserve School at Exeter to re-fuel. I strolled into Flying Control at Exeter in a pair of brown corduroy trousers and a white shirt, having left my flying overalls and helmet in the aircraft as it was a hot day. The RAF Officer looked at me and nearly went through the ceiling. 'What the hell do you think you are doing in one of His Majesty's aircraft?'. I told him I was in the RAF Reserve. 'But that doesn't entitle you to fly!' 'Oh yes it does...' I said '...I'm in the Flying Branch' 'Since when have women been allowed in?' he

Peggy with other RAFVR pilots in the Mess at Hamble.

asked sarcastically. 'Since quite a few months..." I replied. '...you should get caught up with your AMO's (Air Ministry Orders)'. I had not been an WAAF Officer for nothing. At this point another officer came in; he looked at me in astonishment. 'Good Lord...' he said '...a woman! I had just said to a friend, seeing you get out of the aircraft, that chap needs a haircut!'. I finally convinced them that in spite of my rather civilian appearance I had, in fact, orders to be where I was.

We were all aircraft-women, nobody had been given an officers' commission. Most of us had similar experiences and we were often the only women amongst a large number of male reservists".

One day an officer from the legal branch of the RAF, who knew Peggy, saw her and they had a drink together. He asked her what she was doing in just an aircraft-woman's uniform. She said 'That's all I am now'. He said to her 'You are still an officer in the WAAF Reserve, they cannot possibly do this to you'. She replied 'They appear to have done it, and I'm not grumbling. The main thing is that at last they have allowed women into the flying branch of the RAF even if it is only the reserve'.

Peggy continues:

'Eventually they came to the conclusion that as some of us had been WAAF Officers before, something must be done about it. Accordingly, we got an invitation to join a course at Hawkinge with a view to being instructed as officers. I could have got an exemption, but decided to go along, as it would mean a very pleasant fortnights' re-union. Here I found my former CO, Margot Gore, Joy Ferguson and Freydis Leaf, all from the Hamble Pool, amongst others. It was great fun and we did a lot of reminiscing and comparing notes as to what we had been doing since. We were given much the same instruction as I had on my course at Loughborough some years previously. I still had a neatly kept notebook of these, so only had to add a few factors on the things that were new . or had been changed, with the result that I had very little work to do, and it was therefore a very pleasant fortnights' holiday.

Amongst other things, we had a lecture on how to behave in RAF Officers' Messes. I don't think they realised that we had all of us been honorary members of the RAF and Naval Officers' Messes for some years!. Through discussions with others, I began to realise that it was quite possible for us to now get a commercial licence without much expense, which might open the way to jobs in civilian flying.

I determined to work on this and did as much training as possible in the Reserve on instruments and night flying, both of which were required for commercial licences. We were all very lucky at Hamble, as we had two Link Trainers at our disposal. These were simulated aircraft in a room on the ground where you had all the wireless and navigational aids which were controlled by an instructor outside. The course you flew was plotted automatically by a pen on a tracing at the control table. This meant you could learn and practice various means of instrument approaches and landings without actually being in the air. Hamble, as well as being the home of the

RAFVR, had also gone back to its original status of being Air Service Training, the university of the air, which it had been before the war.

I enquired whether they would accept me for a commercial pilots' course. They told me that this was a three year course. When I told them that I already had the necessary flying hours and quite a lot of the technical knowledge required, they said that if I worked hard I could do the Ground School work in about three months. I would have to find my own accommodation as they did not cater for women and I would have, in most cases individual lessons. The temptation was too great. I found that the next examination that I could reasonably take would be in November. Accordingly, I booked in with AST to start there in September"

Peggy gave up her riding school and kept only her favourite horse. She did her annual training with the RAFVR in August, concentrating as much as possible on instrument flying and night flying as possible and spending ground time on the Link Trainer and studying meteorology. She found local digs, thanks to Suzanne Chapman who had been there before her, within easy walking distance of the airfield. In September, she started on the ground syllabus with AST Hamble and took and passed her commercial licence exam in November.

It was all very well having a licence, but getting a job with it was another matter. Breaking into the world of commercial flying for a woman at that time was no easy task. British Overseas Airways Corporation were wanting pilots for their expanding programme and Peggy applied, giving her flying time in ATA, her age, commercial licence details, name and initials. BOAC accepted her, subject to a medical by their doctor, and fixed an appointment for this. When she arrived, the doctor said 'we are not doing hostesses today'. When Peggy replied she was a pilot, he said 'There must be some mistake...' and promptly got on the telephone and said to whoever was at the other end '... Do you realise that this applicant is a WOMAN?' Of course they did'nt and he refused to give her a medical and said that she would hear from them. She did; in a letter which said 'It is not the policy of the company to employ women' and thanking her for her application, they enclosed a paltry sum to cover her train fare to and from the Medical Section.

Peggy took a temporary job with an advertising company in London and continued to apply to every possible advertisement in the flying journals and writing to various clubs. In the spring she applied and got a weeks leave, spending it on a flying instructors' course at White Waltham under Joan Hughes, who had followed up her ATA instructing by doing the same in civilian life. After a flying test at Fairoaks, Peggy got her instructors' endorsement as 'Assistant Instructor'.

Aimee de Neve, who had married again in 1945 and returned to her birthplace of Sri Lanka at the beginning of 1946, found an ancient Mk.V Spitfire lined up for her to fly at Katauneyake Airport. 'It was quite terrifying! I also did some private flying on Austers and had to force-land one on a beach'. She married a Norwegian Naval Officer, who had a wealthy brother in Norway who loved to fly over the mountains and fiords around the West Coast. He had a farm near Ulvik. "We went up in any small aircraft available, looking for his sheep. Rather hazardous, but great fun! I did think about flying commercially at one time, and had the opportunity to do so in South America, but decided against it on account of the family".

She had three children in 1946, 1949 and 1953. Her eldest son, living in Denver, Colorado financed his mother to fly occasionally at Colorado Springs. 'I did some gliding there too. I was taught by an ex RAF Officer who lived in a hangar on the outskirts of the field'.

Pat Provis, who also got married after the war, did no flying for 44 years! She then went up with an instructor in Cornwall (who had less hours than her) and found that she had not forgotten how to fly; like swimming or riding a bicycle, once you have learnt it, it always is there; ones reactions are automatic. Even a strange type made no difference. It was her first flight in a nose-wheel aircraft!

June Farquhar was married soon after the war and had three children. She got involved helping her husband in business and only did some occasional flying for fun at local flying clubs:

"I finally decided it was not worth hanging on to tacky circuits and bumps after flying such super aircraft. Yes, there are times when I dream of being up in the sky alone and totally happy! Do you recall how all earthly troubles would drop away once airborne?"

Frankie Rudge, who had got married while she was in ATA and became Mrs Horsburgh, returned to Canada and had one son who, unfortunately, was killed in an accident. Later, she came back to England and lives in Devon. She had done no flying since the war, but is thinking about it now!

Peggy joined the Guild of Airline Pilots and Navigators which, with her commercial licence she was now eligible for and, at one of their meetings was describing to a friend her attempts to get into the airlines, unaware that the gentleman standing next to her was a journalist. The next day a terrible photograph of her, in a flowery hat taken at a recent wedding was published in a newspaper with the caption 'She wants to be Britain's first airline pilot!'.

"This unsought publicity brought me a sheaf of letters, some of which were very funny. One said 'You have a cheek! I do not know what England is coming to. Anyone flying with you should have their head examined'. Nobody offered me a job however."

At last, to her surprise, she was asked down for an interview at a club on the Isle of Wight. The Chief flying Instructor (CFI) there was an RAF Wing Commander. He told her that the Club Directors were against a woman

She Wants To Be Airline Pilot

One of the newspaper articles (luckily this time at least with an aircraft) that brought much unwanted publicity to Peggy

Teaching at the Central School of Flying at Elstree Aerodrome, Mrs. Peggy Grace wants to be Britain's first woman airline pilot. Five times she has applied to B.O.A.C. and B.E.A. and each time been refused. Mrs. Grace says " Women fly airliners in Russia and Australia, why not in Britain ? " She is a member of the Guild of Air Pilots.

pilot, but with the very small salary they could afford, they could either get a good woman pilot or a bad male one - that is, one that was found not acceptable to the airlines. He knew, from personal experience, the record of the ATA women pilots. The result was she was accepted on trial, and gave notice at her job in London. Her boss asked her why she wanted to leave and she said it was to take up a flying job. "He asked how much I would be paid, and I said Eight pounds a week. 'But you are getting much more than that here, and we could increase it to £20 a week". "It's not a question of money..." she told him."I just want to fly". "Then you are crazy" came the reply.

She left her flat in London and moved to Bembridge for the summer. 'If the airlines wouldn't have me, then club flying was the next best thing, and it was to give me an awful lot of future enjoyment'.

"Geoff Thomas was an extremely nice CFI and I shall always be grateful to him for giving me my first start in civil aviation. I arrived there just in time to help them over the Whit weekend, when they were having a visitors day and flying display - they were busy. I spent two days giving joyrides and after the weekend Geoff told me he was taking two days off as there was nothing booked and they didn't expect to be busy. I was left alone and in charge.

The first morning an RAF Instructor appeared at the flying club. He was a jet instructor and wanted to hire a Tiger Moth to take his mother up for her first flight. He had already flown the Tiger the day before. I told him it was alright for him to have it, but as it had not flown before that day, the engine would need warming up. His mother climbed into the front cockpit and I helped her adjust the safety straps, which were of the Sutton Harness type. Fortunately I fastened them fairly tightly. Leaving one of the mechanics to swing the prop, I went back to the clubhouse where some people were enquiring about flying lessons.

Whilst I was talking to them, I heard the Tiger Moth

take off and the thought went through my mind that it was rather quick - the engine had not had time to warm up. A minute later the mechanic rushed in, as white as a sheet. 'The Moth has crashed in the road!' I jumped into the car and drove quickly up the hill. The aircraft was in the field on the other side of the road, and the pilot was already out with a cut head. He was helping his mother out who, fortunately was not badly hurt, apart from a few minor cuts. Being an elderly lady, she was of course, very badly shaken. The ambulance soon appeared and they were both taken to hospital".

Geoff Thomas was not on the telephone, and lived some distance from the airfield. Peggy had to deal with all the formalities, remember the accident procedure, write out reports, stave off the Press and a mass of holiday-makers that came to 'have a look'.

The next day she arrived at the airfield to find a young boy waiting for her:

"He showed me his logbook, which recorded that he had learned to fly at Eastleigh and his solo hours were signed out by his instructor, whom I knew personally and who was very good. I told him that he would have to have some dual before going solo as Bembridge was smaller and more difficult than Eastleigh. He agreed and did four very good circuits and landings with me, so I sent him off, telling him to keep in sight of the airfield and practice turns etc. (he had not yet got his private pilots' licence).

The phone rang in the office and when I came out there was no sign of him. Half an hour later there was still no Auster. I was not worried as he had petrol for one and a half hours - I thought that he had decided to fly around the island. I rang the three other airfields on the island in case he had landed there by mistake - no news. I was now worried and rang Eastleigh. His instructor there told me that he had been suspended from flying there as he had beaten up a cricket pitch when flying solo and a man there had died of heart failure!. This was devastating news, and I advised Air/Sea Rescue. A bit later the police rang through; the aircraft had landed safely at a disused airfield in the New Forest. A club member flew me over in his aircraft, with a spare can of petrol just in case. After we landed I asked what happened. He said he was depressed and had wanted to commit suicide - he had intended to dive his aircraft at full throttle into the sea!. He changed his mind at the last moment and on pulling out of the dive could not locate his position as it was hazy - he thought the Hampshire coast was the Island. When he realised he was lost he landed at the nearest airfield, but found it was deserted and had a long way to go to the nearest habitation.

I flew him back to Bembridge. As I taxied in, Geoff and his wife drove up in their car. 'Everything going alright?' he asked with a cheerful smile. 'Hardly that. The Tiger Moth has crashed and I've just brought a pupil in who wanted to commit suicide'. I gave him the details.

Geoff was quite ruthless. 'You are a selfish young man' he told him. 'You don't stop to think about other people. Besides killing yourself, you want to rob us of an aircraft and cause a lot of people to spend time and money searching for you all over the place, and picking up the bits if they find them. If you must commit suicide, which is a very stupid thing to do anyway, put your head in a gas oven - it causes a lot less trouble and does the job just as well'.

I thought to myself, this probably is the right way, psychologically, to deal with a case like this, but I would need a lot more experience before I could adopt such a matter of fact attitude. Geoff followed this up with a much more kinder and more fatherly talk with the boy, which I thought probably helped him a lot.

This initial rather dramatic couple of days as flying instructor made me wonder if I had bitten off more than I could chew; but the normal routine proved afterwards to be much less demanding on the nerves, and I thoroughly enjoyed my subsequent days at Bembridge.

At the end of summer, flying dropped off. As my

engagement had only been temporary, I was offered a job instructing at Cowes Airport for a month, after which I returned home to see my mother and have a short holiday. There was not much doing in club flying during the winter, but I was taken on as a part-time weekend instructor at Elstree, where the school was run by David Cotter, a former ATA pilot.

I went there several weekends and helped out. Then I applied for a job with a flying club in Yorkshire and was told to come up. In Yorkshire they were less prejudiced against women, as Suzanne Chapman had been instructing at Sherburne very successfully, and they had grown used to the idea. I arrived at West Hartlepool, which I found an extremely nice and friendly club, only to find that they expected me to act as CFI!. I pointed out the fact that I only had an Assistant Instructors' rating, which did not authorise me to take sole charge of a flying school. I helped them out, but told them I could not consider staying there permanently without a CFI, as I only risked getting myself in trouble.

This was brought home to me by the fact that on one day Sherburne were having an 'At Home', and our club pilots had been invited over. Several had flown there and while they were on the ground the weather had deteriorated considerably. Snowstorms were coming in from the North Sea. I rang the club at Sherburne and suggested that our pilots had better return if they wanted to get back that night, or stop where they were. Within an hour some were back, but two were still missing. I rang the club again, and they said that both of them had taken off. I thought, if they ran into bad weather, they could turn around and land back at Sherburne.

The weather got worse, and snowstorms reached the edge of the airfield. Suddenly, I heard an aircraft and rushed to get the 'Véry' Pistol. I fired off several white and green flares, but the pilot obviously did not see them. He missed the airfield and I could hear the aircraft going out to sea. Once again I was worried and stood outside by the signals square, listening and looking. After a bit I heard the aircraft returning. Again I fired lights, but again he was too far away to see them. At this moment I got a telephone call from the Police. They told me that one aircraft was down in a field and would be staying there the night. A second call said that the other aircraft was also down in a field, slightly damaged owing to an unseen ditch, but the pilot and his three child passengers were uninjured. I breathed a sigh of relief and, loading my car with ropes and pickets, drove out in the snowstorm to make the aircraft secure for the night and pick up the pilots"

She told the club Directors that she could not stay there and instruct with her Assistant Instructor's Endorsement unless they got a fully licensed instructor. She very reluctantly said goodbye to West Hartlepool, where she had received great hospitality, and accepted a full time job instructing at Elstree.

Annual leave having to be taken in January, when there was least flying training, she flew out to North Africa and the Sahara in an Auster. She also bought and delivered a Proctor to a client in Madrid and bought herself a small Taylorcraft Auster for £150, which she could keep and have serviced at the club in exchange for its use by the club for instructing. This was an ideal arrangement as it meant that she had an aircraft to use on her days off and could also attend air rallies and competitions.

The following year the school moved to Gatwick, which was still then a large grass airfield, ideal for instruction and easily reached by train from London. It was a Customs Airport even then, which meant that it was easy to arrange flights to France for the day. In 1952, the club went over in force to the Tours Air Rally with five aircraft, and came back laden with three large cups and innumerable bottles of champagne and wine, having won all the major prizes. Peggy also took part in the 'Daily Express' air races at this period, also winning a very welcome amount of prize money.

To the victors, the spoils! Above: Peggy receiving her prize at the end
of the 'Daily Express' Air Race at Shoreham on 6 August 1951.
Below: Peggy (with Trophy) and cases of Champagne at the Tours
International Air Rally on 6 July 1952.

At the end of the year she remarried, and flew her Auster out to Switzerland where her husband was working. After four miscarriages, she renewed her licences and bought and flew the first aircraft for the Innsbruck Flying Club, and remained as instructor at Innsbruck for three years. Suzanne Chapman came out to Austria with a 'Speaking Aircraft' and visited her.

Suzanne did some 'sky shouting' for a local circus in the Tyrol for their publicity, until local farmers complained it frightened their cows, so she had to stop!

Peggy organised two international air rallies at Innsbruck before moving to Kitzbuhel and opening a small airstrip there for pleasure flights. This she did in partnership with George Cochrane, an Englishman living there. They bought a four-seater Auster and did flights locally around the villages, and further afield around the Kaiser Mountains and over the glaciers of the Tauern - incredibly beautiful flights, but always at a safe height so that a valley could be reached in a glide in the event of an engine failure. This. fortunately never happened.

At 74, she has let her licences lapse. but still goes flying whenever the opportunity presents itself. 'Even as a passenger, I love seeing the infinite variety and

Peggy in front of the nose of her pleasure-flying Auster V OE-DBZ in the misty Austrian Alps during July 1960.

colouring of the clouds, the circular rainbows with the aircraft outlined in the centre, the tall pillars of cumulus, which are just black clouds on the ground".

And of the others...?

Suzanne Chapman decided to return to the WAAF when ATA closed down and took her former rank of Section Officer at RAF Station Madley, where she was Technical Equipment Officer. This proved to have certain advantages as, when she resigned a year later, she received an educational grant from the RAF to help her train for a commercial licence with AST. By the end of 1947, she passed both her Commercial Pilots and 1st Class Navigators exams and could start immediately in a flying job that had been offered in Hereford.

In the ATA she had been the second WAAF to qualify on Class II aircraft and had ferried a total of 25 different types, thus beating both Peggy and Pooh, who had a total of 19 types each. She just missed the last conversion course on Class III (Twin engined types), but converted to these at Hereford, where she flew DH Rapides and the Percival Q.6. She was doing mostly taxi-work, joy-riding and aerial photography.

In 1949, she joined the RAFVR (Flying) at Wolverhampton, where she did an Instructors' course in 1950, and got her RAF wings in 1951. After a spell out into family life (she got married and had a daughter) she joined Island Air Services, who at the time had the joy-riding concession at London's Heathrow Airport. This operation was so successful that on one day she clocked 31 landings in a Rapide; the queue for pleasure flights was continuous.

In 1955 she joined the 'Talking Aeroplane Co' and flew an Auster fitted with a Tannoy speaker under each wing. Flights were made whereever contracts for advertising by words from the sky could be obtained.

In 1957 she went back to instructing at Swansea, where she became CFI and an approved instructor for

RAF Cadets.

She re-married and gave up her flying licences in 1969, having achieved a total of 3,462 hours recorded in her log-books; actually quite a few more, as flying instructors were often careless about entering every flight after they had passed 2000 hours. She now instructs Scuba Diving and her main hobby is bird watching.

Monique Agazarian (affectionately known to most of her friends as 'Aggie') was not actually in the WAAF, but in their more senior and respected service, Princess Mary's RAF Nursing Service. She had two brothers in the RAF and one in Special Operations, and was very keen to fly herself. She put in an application as soon as she heard that ATA would be training a few pilots ab initio, and was accepted and started training on the course before the 17 WAAF came in and did exactly the same training, flying her first Spitfire in June 1944. After her Class III conversion course, she was posted to Hamble, where she shared a cottage with Sheila Garratt (the glamorous American), Mary and Peggy. When Hamble closed she was posted to Hawarden for the final two months and, determined to go on flying, she worked for her commercial licence and got it in 1946. She joined a private air company which had been started by Daughleigh Hills-Grove-Hills, based at St Mary's in the Isles of Scilly, called Island Air Services.

Monique:
"As London Manager, I flew the second Proctor, which was partly hired by Elstree, particularly during the the flower season, flying daffodils from the Scillies to the Mainland (fifty boxes per flight!) and charter flights throughout the UK

and Europe.

Later that same year, Island Air Services opened a base at Croydon, with office, handling staff and engineering facilities. Business literally 'took off' and Cecile Power, who had also been at Hamble with me, joined us. Our flights were mostly jockeys to and from race meetings in the UK, business and holiday taxi-flights to France, the Low Countries, Spain, Switzerland and Italy. The first Rapide was bought and throughout the summer I operated between Croydon and Jersey/Guernsey, carrying six passengers three times a day and, of course the Scillies on charter and the flower service. We had two crew on the International flights, myself and a Radio Operator.

Island Air Services (London) was made into a limited company. I was Chief Pilot and Chairman, with Ray Rendall and John Helps as Pilot co-Directors. We continued to operate three trips a day at weekends on the Channel Islands run, as well as charters throughout Europe and UK on

Newspaper deliveries, press photography and all that, with a permanent strength of four pilots, radio operators and three Rapides. By then we had our own Engineering base at Croydon. Additional Rapides with part-time

DH89 Rapide G-AGUF, flagship of the IAS fleet at Croydon.

crews were leased to deal with the day trips to the French resorts, foreign race meetings and the extra newspaper deliveries during strikes.

We obtained a contract for operating pleasure flights from Northolt, then Heathrow. This operation became so successful that we leased additional Rapides, an Anson, a Consul and even, one day, an Ambassador from BEA!

I negotiated an Associate Agreement with BEA to operate a scheduled service between Shoreham and Deauville and this daily service started on 1 July 1950. Meanwhile we also continued to operate charter flights from both Croydon and Heathrow. It is amusing to note that the first time 1000 movements were logged in a day at Heathrow was when we were running pleasure flights there!

Veronica Volkersz was employed by IAS until she left to fly Mosquitoes at Lambedr. Suzanne Chapman was also employed for one summer at Heathrow until she moved on to be an instructor.

Pleasure flights were discontinued at London Airport in 1959 owing to the rapidly increasing traffic. The demand for small charters also came to an end and I went to the Lebanon and only flew privately until my return to the UK, when I again flew commercially freelance on light twins for various operators on UK and European charters"

This rather terse account of a successful business career in aviation leaves out the fact that she also found time to get married and produce three charming daughters and bring them up most effectively, proving that it can be done! She later joined Graeme Percival in teaching current airway flying on flight simulators and took over the company, Air Training Services when he died in 1976.

Since then she has been training both ab initio and qualified pilots, and is approved by the Civil Aviation Authority for the full instrument rating course. In addition, she has also written a very clear and easily understood text book, called *'Instrument Flying and background to the Instrument and IMC Ratings'* which has proved extremely popular. She still holds today (1992) a current Commercial Pilots Licence with Instrument rating!

A friend writes of her "A seemingly frivolous and fun-loving nature, plus a wicked sense of humour, in fact disguises a character of great discernment and good judgement".

The ATA training proved that women could fly aircraft as well as men; and also instruct as well. However, the fact remains that out of the 17 WAAF so trained and really keen to fly, only Suzanne and Peggy went on to make a career out of flying. All except one got married, or re-married, which makes one wonder if women are a good proposition for the airlines. Now that they can no longer say '..it is not the policy of the company to employ women', many women today are flying as Captains or First Officers of large passenger aircraft - but how many will drop out when they get married and have a family?. The womans place may really be in the home!

Many will always want to fly though, and will not let anything stop them.

June:

"There is no denying, we lived in a superb era, and were so very fortunate to be paid for doing a job that we would have given anything under the sun to do. What a fantastic training and how confident it made us all. I still marvel at the fact one could climb into a totally unknown aircraft, thumb through our Pilots Handling Notes, spend a little while familiarising oneself with the layout of the aircraft and HTT MPP FGG FUST - that cockpit drill is still in my memory!. Then away into the wide blue yonder! Lucky, lucky us".